The Legitimacy to Effectively Govern

Andy Sibbald

The Legitimacy to Effectively Govern

Published in Canada by Lunatic Publishing
Copyright @ 2023 by Andy Sibbald

Please address queries to:
Lunatic Publishing
#105, 1130 Pandora Avenue
Victoria, BC Canada
V8V 3R1

ISBN: 9798387179334

Cover design and art by Iryna Spica

Printed and bound with KDP

My Thanks to

*Iryna Spica for the cover art
and her proofreading, layout and design work*

Nipi and Jon for your ongoing encouragement

Other Books by Andy Sibbald

FOR ADULTS

Grease My Hooves: Politics in Canada

Wen Shen: The Queen of Wu Kang

One Soldier's Journey: The Canadian Forestry Corps

The Catholic Abuse of Filipino Women

Prejudice, Racism, Exclusion and Exploitation

The Quest for Social Responsibility

On the Brink

Ongoing Genocide and Canada's Aboriginal People

The Rejection of Reality: QAnon to Election Fraud

When the Left was Right

Religion, Politics and Power

The Joys of Travel

THE 101 SERIES

Dirty Contracting 101

Yellow Journalism 101

Self-Serving Religion 101

COVID-19 101

Disorganized Crime 101

Pink Trash 101

Canadian Politics 101

Public Institutions 101

THE EVERY VILLAGE NEEDS AND IDIOT

Ms. Stinky Does Esquimalt

The Quack of Quadra Village

Uncle Ponzi: The Oaf of Oak Bay

The Quack of Quadra Village

The Langford Lush

"Foxy" Visits Mongolia

The Jackass of James Bay

The Dockside Green Dummy

Luna Tick: The Witch of Vic West

Ms. Stinky Goes to the Slammer

The Fernwood Fanatic

The Greater Esquimalt Drunken Seagulls

Tofino to Tokyo

The Quack of Quadra Village

FOR TEENS

Ishigaq: The Quest for Home

Ishigaq: Nipster's Magical Cane

Ishigaq: Following Nipster's Dream

Table of Contents

Preamble. 1

I Can Do the Job 13

Democracy, Trust and Legitimacy . . . 26

Wars and Natural Disasters 49

Insight, or Lack Thereof 72

Passive Aggressive Politics Canadian Style . 83

Someone Else's Fault 97

What Now? 126

Avoiding the Obvious 137

The Party With No Platform 148

Just the Facts. 169

Incompetence, Discontent and

Rise of the Right 178

Government's Role in Law Enforcement . . 193

Where to From Here? 217

Stopping the Bleeding 227

Preamble

In political science, **legitimacy** is the right and acceptance of an authority, usually a governing law or a regime. Whereas *authority* denotes a specific position in an established government, the term *legitimacy* denotes a system of government—wherein *government* denotes "sphere of influence". An authority viewed as legitimate often has the right and justification to exercise power. Political legitimacy is considered a basic condition for governing, without which a government will suffer legislative deadlock(s) and collapse. In political systems where this is not the case, unpopular regimes survive because they are considered legitimate by a small, influential elite.[1]

---

1   Wikipedia. *Legitimacy (political)*. January 31, 2022.

Just before we get started it is important that you, the reader, can choose to use the term credibility interchangeably with legitimacy throughout this book. The term legitimacy is used to mean far more than winning an election and therefore having the legitimacy to govern. In a democracy people are only governed because they are willing to accept authority. There are increasingly less people willing to accept this authority and this book explores the reasons why.

We are at a point where major societal changes are occurring. Many people are angry and there have been situations bordering on lawlessness, like the anti-vaccination mandate truck convoy in Ottawa and the January 6 attempted coup in Washington. An increasing number of people have little respect for the government and the law. Either that, or people have become emboldened by the rhetoric of the far-right in the United States. We know there is a problem when the number of unhappy people showing up for demonstrations far outnumber the police and pose a potential threat to the people and communities where the demonstrations occur. When injunctions are provided by the courts to cease the demonstration, these have been ignored by some. People arrive at highways, bridges and elsewhere and unlawfully block traffic. This may include blocking ambulances, fire trucks and other emergency vehicles. Then there are the professional demonstrators that are often funded through organizations in other countries who wish to create political unrest. Professional demonstrators move from one cause to the next and the cause is often immaterial to them. These career demonstrators are paid with donations from people who are passionate about various causes. You know there is a problem when a so-called First Nations demonstration includes one First Nation's individual and a host of professional white demonstrators. While they do their job, they have no qualms about blocking you from getting to yours. It is another aggravation and there is a collective, "what the Hell is going on"? Perhaps you supported the cause when it involved picket signs and people walking around beside the road but now that you cannot get to work on time you are losing sympathy and are angry. You debate getting out of your car but think better of it. You wonder where the police are. You ask yourself if the demonstrators really think that making your life more difficult will make you want to save some penguin colony in Argentina. Probably not, but it has managed to make you extremely angry. The majority of the people in the demonstration have just come from a save the whales event, and a demonstration to save old growth forests. None have ever seen a penguin, let alone been to Argentina, but they wave their flags, impede honest citizens trying to get to work and yell at people as if it is a capital crime to be less concerned about penguins, no one has seen, than it is about being late for work. You are angry and who can blame you?

When you get to work you mention the demonstration and apologize to your boss for being late to. A colleague overhears the conversation and decides to intervene and give you a lecture about the right to demonstrate in both Canada and the United States. You take a deep breath and point out that you are aware of this and that you support peaceful demonstrations but not ones that are highly disruptive and hurt the economy. Before your colleague can further his lecture you wisely leave the area and get to work, wondering if tomorrow morning will be more of the same. Meanwhile people in other demonstrations with legitimate causes are being smeared by those who do not share their views. Truckers are refusing to stop blocking international borders and stores are becoming alarmingly low on food and other essentials. Workers in the auto industry are being laid off, albeit temporarily because their plants cannot get essential parts. When demonstrations cost Canadians millions of dollars and interfere with the supply chain, enough is enough! When people attack the Capitol in Washington, enough is enough! Of course, it may have been enough for you and I, but perhaps that just illustrates how we would be politically aligned when a genocide/civil war breaks out in the United States and overflows into Canada. This is starting to appear inevitable as I watch the mass right-wing stupidity in the United States. Millions of people in the United States and Canada are living in fantasy lands of conspiracy theories that they have come to believe are reality. People with doctorates and lifetimes of scientific work have been reduced to the equivalent of people with grade six who "have done their own research" on social media. Technology used to be controlled by man but none of us can keep up with the rapid developments on so many different fronts. We have no idea what all these incremental increases in technology will do, or how they will collectively interact. Perhaps it is like getting many different bottles of pills and without reading anything about the drugs, or how they interact, taking a handful of them and hoping for the best. Like with all the scientists, there is no overall plan or understanding about how all the new technologies will interact. So, we hold our breath and hope that they will be the saviour for the planet and not the cause of its demise. Perhaps,

I should check on Facebook, or Twitter because no doubt there is an expert on there with grade six who can predict the future, and if I am really lucky, he or she may sell me some elixir to protect me from future technological advancements, a la Jim Baker.

We see grocery and accommodation prices rising rapidly but our wages and pensions are not. All around me condos are replacing older stores, apartments and the jobs and incomes that went with them. Why? So that dirty money can be laundered and so that wealthy people can move in and buy up these condos that only outsiders can afford. I know I should move into affordable housing but the city and I differ considerably on what affordable housing means. Then I hear from a person who works in old folks' homes, that living in one of the homes she works in costs $12,000 a month. I wonder if the city considers this affordable housing. I phone the place for fun and ask what it would cost me per month to live there, if I provided my own food and meals. The lady tells me in a serious voice that it would result in my monthly rent dropping by $200. Yes, that changes everything!

Then there was the whole Covid-19 debacle in Canada where the Federal Government did not adopt a tone of trying to help Canadians but adopted one of wanting to punish Canadians. Do you have any idea how much it costs to be quarantined in a hotel near the Vancouver airport for fourteen days? How did the government come up with the figure of a $750,000 fine for non-compliance with quarantine rules? Is this warranted for someone who accidentally forgot to put their mask on? This was all relatively new for Canadians when Covid-19 started. I understand full well the seriousness of failing to wear a mask, or following quarantine rules but when traffic fines for cell phone usage while driving, speeding and drunk driving may offer penalties that are in the hundreds and low thousands of dollars, $750,000 is clearly a penalty that is both excessive and cruel. If you do not think this was unnecessarily punitive and politically motivated ask yourself this; if you had broken the rules would a $2,000, or $25,000 fine be sufficient to modify your behaviour so that you complied with the quarantine rules in the future? Impaired driving is more likely to kill someone and the fine is in the hundreds, or low thousands of dollars. But granny needs a $750,000 fine which will result in her losing everything she owns to send her a message. Do you not think a $200 fine would have given granny the same message without destroying her life and leaving her homeless? Prime Minister Trudeau knew that Canadians supported penalties for Covid-19 violations so he brought in excessive punishments that only his class could afford in an attempt to compensate for his general incompetence and lack of doing little more than talking and talking…

- Canada has imposed strict punishments for those who break its coronavirus rules.

- Everyone entering the country will be required to quarantine except essential workers, like truck drivers.

- Those who don't — or those who get caught not wearing a mask — could face a fine up to $750,000.

The country on Tuesday announced that all travelers entering the country would be required to quarantine themselves for 14 days, even if they aren't showing symptoms of Covid-19. There are "few exceptions," to the rules, the government's public health agency said, besides those who "ensure the continued flow of goods and essential services, or individuals who receive or provide other essential services to Canadians."

Those exempt individuals, like truck drivers, are still required to wear a mask upon entry to the country and while in transit. The rules are punishable by a fine of up to $750,000 or a month in jail, and the government will be conducting spot checks to ensure compliance, it said.[2]

It is pretty difficult to draw any other conclusion than this was an abuse of power and was extremely heavy handed. Canadians generally comply with reasonable rules and laws and I am not sure why the government felt it necessary to basically threaten to hit someone who forgot to put their mask on with a fine that could result in them losing their home, their business and be in debt for the remainder of their lives. As for the fourteen-day quarantine, I suppose those in Prime Minister Trudeau's class can afford fourteen nights in Vancouver airport hotels but few others can. The Covid-19 quarantine rules also begged the question that, if the masks are so good at stopping the spread of the virus along with the vaccines, why can someone wearing a mask who is vaccinated not sit in the back of a cab when arriving in their town and go home to quarantine for fourteen days, rather

____

2   Graham Rapier. Insider. *People entering Canada could face a $750,000 fine if they don't quarantine for 14 days — even if they don't show coronavirus symptoms.* April 18, 2020

than in some expensive hotel? I know of one couple from Nova Scotia where they were initially told they would have to drive past their home to quarantine in a nearby facility. They managed to get an exemption to the quarantine order so that they could quarantine at home but again, you can see the silliness. Meanwhile, the Prime Minister was on television everyday telling us essentially the same thing. He is a drama teacher by trade, so I am sure this was right up his alley. He ultimately concluded that he had been doing such a good job that he would call an election one-and one-half years into a four-year term as Prime Minister. That resulted in Canadians paying $600 million so we could have an almost duplicate Liberal minority government. There were also his three major ethical violations, dressing up in Indian clothing in India, failing to go to a First Nation he had been invited to for the first National Day for Truth and Reconciliation, lying about bringing in a proportional voting system and a host of other embarrassing things for Canadians. My other books discuss these things, so I won't get into them in any depth here.

Governments in democracies must have the legitimacy to govern. The mere fact that people are elected does not provide this. Legitimacy goes beyond being elected. It requires that people accept the government's authority to govern. This means that they have a certain degree of respect for the government, see it is being reasonable, and recognize that it has the right to govern. Legitimacy is gained by compliance with rules and laws and role modelling. Respect and legitimacy, in the context I am using these terms, is earned. Being elected alone provides neither. It is the behaviour of those who are elected which determines whether they have the legitimacy to govern. The problem we have in Canada and the United States is that governments are no longer seen as having the legitimate right to govern. I should mention that this has absolutely nothing to do with former President Trump's Big Lie that the election was stolen from him. It wasn't! This book is not about political parties per se but is about the broader issue of political systems, corruption, abuses and criminal activity that have led us to this point where it is clear that the public sees the Canadian and American governments as having less legitimacy to govern. This in turn has resulted in more aggressive civil unrest and more aggressive responses to it by governments. We are headed to a tipping point because when it gets to the point where there are enough people who see North American governments as lacking the legitimacy to govern through their own doing, we will have a major problem, the likes of which North Americans have not experienced in my lifetime.

The governments in North America would be wise to look internally to find out why there is increased civil disobedience and why these governments are seen to have considerably less legitimacy to govern than previous governments. I wonder if it has ever dawned on our so-called political leaders that the corruption, ethical and legal violations and lying would catch up with them, and that they are playing a significant role in destroying democracy and any credibility these governments may have had. I doubt it because arrogance and a sense of entitlement can lead one to believe that they deserve the respect of the public, when nothing could be further from the truth. Referring to Prime Minister Trudeau as a leader only demonstrates a clear misunderstanding of the term.

I Can Do the Job

Would you think of going down to General Motors and submitting your resume for the vacant Chief Executive Officer, or Chief Financial Officer positions? Would you think that when Bill Gates moves on that you would be the ideal candidate to replace him at Microsoft? No, and neither would I. We are not remotely qualified for positions like that and are smart enough to realize it. These positions require training, education and thought processes at the highest levels. We may be good at what we did for careers but recognize that we simply lack the skill sets required to take on jobs at this level. Unfortunately, in politics one only has to be popular. This is ludicrous when you consider that running a country requires management skills and ideally integrity at the highest levels. It requires leadership skills and an ability to problem solve at the highest level. It also requires ethics, common sense and an ability to inspire and motivate. Let me rephrase this because this is what is required of a leader, and leaders often stay out of politics. We often get people elected who are not leaders, and other than being popular are not remotely qualified to assume the leadership of a country. You and I recognize that we do not have the skill sets required to do an adequate job of running a country, unlike some of our recent political party leaders.

If you were a drama teacher or a mail room worker for an oil company, would you think that you had the ability and intelligence required to run the multi-billion-dollar business called Canada? In fairness to Stephen Harper, unlike Prime Minister Trudeau, he did have a Bachelor's degree and a Master's degree in economics and this is not only significant but highly appropriate for the position of Prime Minister. Most of us, like Harper, had lesser jobs and enjoyed greater success as we gained education, skills and experience.

Justin Trudeau was a Member of Parliament prior to running for leader of the Liberal Party. It is fair to suggest that he was elected to this position primarily because his father, Pierre Trudeau had previously been a Prime Minister. Justin Trudeau is a teacher, yet, he assumed that he was the right person for the job. I am not sure how a teacher assumed that he is Prime Ministerial material but that is precisely what happened, and obviously, very close to a majority of Canadians agreed with him. He did lose the popular vote the last two elections but in Canada the party with the most votes does not necessarily win. To run for office, the following criterion must be met. If you get elected, you may then run for the leadership of the party. If you become the party leader, and your party wins the national election, you will become the Prime Minister of Canada.

Eligibility

The right to run in a federal election is protected by the *Canadian Charter of Rights and Freedoms*. The basic requirements to become a candidate are the following:

- You must be a Canadian citizen.

- You must be at least 18 years old on election day.

- You must not be deemed ineligible under the criteria listed in section 65 of the Act.

- You must submit either a *Nomination Paper* (EC 20010) (paper copy filed at the returning officer's office) or an Online nomination form (filed on the Political

Entities Service Centre portal) along with all required supporting documents. The filing deadline is 21 days before election day at 2:00 p.m. local time.

Note: You may only seek election in a single electoral district at a time, but you do not need to reside in that district.[3]

If you wish to work for Burger King you need the following qualifications. As you can see there are far more written expectations than there are to run for public office in Canada. Popularity alone may result in you becoming the Prime Minister but is not enough to gain a job with Burger King. It is actually reassuring to see what can be expected from a Burger King employee. There are few standards attached to becoming an elected official and that has been blatantly obvious at times. The requirements to become a Burger King team member are as follows.

Position Overview:

The Team Member is responsible for providing exceptional guest service while working closely with the Restaurant Managers and other Team Members to maintain

---

3   Elections Canada. *How to Become a Candidate-Eligibility.* January 27, 2022.

operational standards and procedures. This position operates under the direction of the General Manager, Assistant Managers, and Shift Coordinators. This position has direct interactions with Guests and members of the field operations team.

Summary Of Essential Duties And Responsibilities:

- Greets guests with a smile while receiving orders and processing payments

- Prepares and packages food and drink products

- Responsible for maintaining the cleanliness of the restaurant at all times including dining room, restroom & exterior

- Maintains health and safety standards in work areas

- Unloads and stocks inventory items as needed

- Prompt and regular attendance on assigned shifts

- Follows Burger King uniform and grooming standards and policies

Qualifications And Skills:

- Must be at least sixteen (16) years of age

- Comfortable working in a fast paced environment

- Ability to interact in a positive and professional manner with guests and coworkers

- Willingness to learn all areas of restaurant operations & work multiple stations

- Available to work evenings, weekends and holidays[4]

In the United States the last few Presidents have made me wonder. Ronald Reagan was an actor; George Bush Jr. was not exactly a shining star and Donald Trump has spent half his life in litigation, and has a horrible reputation among many who have done business with him. Nevertheless, there were enough Americans who thought he would be a good choice for President and he was elected. It makes me wonder when I look at politics in Canada and the United States, if like the bureaucrats at the highest levels of government, people who run for the leaderships of parties, and who stand to become the leaders of their countries

---

4   Job Opportunities. *Burger King. Team Member.* 2019.

should have some basic qualifications, and meet some other basic requirements, like having no criminal record for example. As it is, we can elect people who have never seen a balance sheet, have operated their businesses corruptly, know nothing about the political system, and nothing about governance and leadership. It would be nice if they knew something about ethics and were seen to have integrity. It is helpful in any job to understand one's limitations. I mean, think about it; to work at a burger joint you may have to provide a resume and have three interviews because you will be handling money and need to be personally suited to the position you have applied for. To be a politician you need a bunch of signatures and some cash. I could get a nomination sheet filled out down the street by the homeless people there. Cash, if one knows where to look, and knows which corporations will be seeking support for various corporate goals cannot be that difficult to find, given an in. You don't require any education, skills, or training to become the Prime Minister of Canada, or the President of the United States and the wage is far better than what others who are totally unqualified for their positions, might expect to receive as compensation.

If you were down at the beach and someone who you thought had no credibility, based on their previous comments and behaviour told you that you needed to vacate the beach immediately, due to a tsunami being reported, would you leave the beach? Perhaps you would ignore the person, or seek out a more reliable source, if in the past the person had exaggerated, or lied to you. Or perhaps you would just tune them out and ignore them due to their total lack of credibility. Is this not to some degree what happens with national leaders who have had repeated ethical violations, histories of corruption, lying and acting primarily out of self-interest. Do we not tune them out because we have come to believe listening to them, due to their lack of credibility, is a waste of time? We may feel we would be better to seek someone with more credibility to provide us with our information? When millions of your countrymen get to a point where they see their national leader as having no credibility, they then lack the legitimacy to govern, whether they were elected, or not. Respect is earned and when it is lost due to ongoing abuses, it is exceedingly difficult to recapture.

I never respected my boss because she was my boss. That was not enough of a reason. I respected my boss because of her competence, integrity, ethics, the way she treated me and others, and for a host of other reasons. Her position alone did not mean that she automatically possessed these qualities. She earned my respect and trust and we remain friends because of who she is and not because of a position she held.

This is something lost on a lot of leaders. If I were Prime Minister Trudeau, I would be tremendously embarrassed to be out in public after two major ethical violations, and would not wonder why people do not want to listen to me and don't trust me. Nor should I presume to know what is best for the people of the country when clearly, I have some serious issues around credibility, integrity and common sense. I felt this way when the Prime Minister chose to tell people on a daily basis what was being done about Covid-19. Rightly, or wrongly I had just hoped he would be quiet and was appalled that he was willing to seek frequent media attention after two major ethical violations, playing Mr. Costumes in India, using tax money for his holiday that involved one meeting over a week, and the debacle with the convicted murderer and the state dinner. This caused tremendous embarrassment for Canadians, but I suspect the Prime Minister was too arrogant for this to register. So, when Covid-19 came along it was time for more theatrics and attention seeking since he had done so little of what he said he would do, and people were tired of him talking a good game but doing little.

There were many elements to the trucker convoy to protest vaccine mandates. The protest involving the truckers was initially fine but right-wing elements got involved and the protest soon turned ugly. That aside, I wonder if Trudeau would have felt the need to invoke the Emergencies Act to deal with the blockades and border closures, if he was taken seriously and listened too. I also wonder if his hiding during this episode emboldened the right-wing elements that were causing the majority of the problems. Certainly, running away does not show leadership and nor does it build respect.

The presumption we tend to make in democracies is that we would only elect those who are qualified to do the job. The problem is that the only qualification for the job is to be popular. Using that criterion, we do elect qualified leaders but what does popularity have to do with having the capability to manage a multi-billion-dollar corporation? Would Canadian Tire, or the Canadian Imperial Bank of Commerce hire someone as their Chief Executive Officer because they are popular. Certainly, it may help but the successful candidates will have references from those who can speak to their competence, reams of paper qualifications, likely from the finest schools and years of experience. Moving up through the ranks of a political party, or having family members involved in politics may teach one a great deal about various political jobs, but it does not necessarily teach them about economics, finance, diplomacy, ethics, common sense, the ability to manage, or how to lead competently, and to problem solve at the highest levels. God knows how many of us have seen people who have worked in jobs for years be elevated to management positions who had no idea how to manage people, or the operation they became in charge of. So, it is fine to say that in a democracy we will hire (elect) people who are qualified but isn't it a bit like saying we will hire the pool boy to fix the electrical problem. The set of skills required to rise in a political party are not the set of skills required to competently run the country. Should we be surprised when the pool boy gets a nasty jolt of electricity and is unable to complete the job? Should we be surprised when we often get incompetent people in politics? Being popular is not a skill at all but is rather a personal attribute. Aside from the ideal that anyone can run in a democracy, and this is hugely important, would it be too problematic to require that our political leaders at minimum have a Bachelor's degree in a subject relevant to running a country. If we want to become a nurse, or social worker we are required to have a degree, and those that want to manage a billion-dollar operation should at least have a relevant degree, at absolute minimum. I want to know that I am voting for someone who has at least made an effort to prepare themselves for the job of Prime Minister in the same way we expect a janitor to possess certain knowledge, experience and skills. From that perspective is it too much to ask that those wishing to become the Prime Minister, like those wishing to work at Burger King, possess certain basic qualifications? I don't think so, and if there were basic qualifications, we may find that we get better Prime Ministers. In closing, can you think of any other job where there is such a disconnect between what you need (popularity) to get the job, and what you require to do the job (management, accounting economics, diplomacy, integrity etc.) as the Prime Minister of Canada and the President of the United States? Next time you are unhappy with the job the Prime Minister, or President is doing, look into their qualifications and background and you will understand why. Prime Minister Trudeau is a drama teacher who thought he could competently fulfil the duties of the Canadian Prime Minister. All he required to get this position was to be eighteen and popular. Even in terms of the requirement that he be popular, he did not win the popular vote. So, we end up with a Prime

Minister who is not even popular, aside from his lack of any other qualifications to do the job. Somehow, he apparently thought that he was qualified, perhaps because his father was a former Prime Minister. Last time I checked there were no apprenticeship programs to become the Prime Minister so, we have ended up with a drama teacher with a love for power and the desire to punish fellow Canadians with unnecessarily strict and in many cases expensive, punitive Covid-19 rules that restrict my class, but not his of course. Do I think Justin Trudeau has the legitimacy to govern? No, but then he won the election according to the rules and can legally govern.

Ironically, Prime Minister Trudeau's ideology and mine align far more closely than mine with the Conservative party. That fails to make me think that he is a good leader because, regardless of one's ideology, competence is demonstrated through behaviour, rather than talk.

Democracy, Trust and Legitimacy

There are those who seem to think that because one attains a position, they should immediately be afforded respect, should be assumed to be honest, possess integrity, be intelligent and possess common sense. I think you would agree that some people possess these attributes, while there are others who only possess a portion of them, or none of them. You will also likely agree that most must be demonstrated in order that we develop things like trust and respect for a person's judgment, integrity and intelligence. Democracies are based on trust. When a person struggles to demonstrate these qualities and then shows that they have no integrity, why should they be afforded any respect. There are many "leaders" that warrant no respect. The world is full of them at present and the populist leaders and people like Trump, Putin, Trudeau and Boris Johnson do not deserve our respect.

Just watching these people in action, along with people like the leaders of Brazil and India tell me that populist leaders are often not leaders at all and operate on a self-serving basis to the exclusion of all else. Why would we think that a leader who has committed war crimes has the legitimacy to govern, or a dictator like Putin who has jailed his predominant rival.

In North American culture we tend to assume things about people who we actually know nothing about. We think we know the characters of the athletes and movie stars we see on television and think we know a fair bit about the politicians we elect. Then we see that the nice actor we saw on one of our favourite television shows has sexually assaulted someone and we cannot believe it. But why, when all we know is the person portrayed in a program we like to watch. We put people, often undeservedly, on pedestals, and then they fall. Like the NFL quarterback who pretended he was vaccinated. Later it was found out that he wasn't vaccinated at all, in spite of him having close interactions with his teammates. Yes, a great player but an unpleasant human being. So, we elect politicians who we assume will do the right thing and honour the oaths they took to defend the Constitution and the values therein. Elections are all about portraying an appealing image that the public will like. That is why it comes as a great shock when we find out that the Republican party has no interest in democracy. When the public elected Republican politicians they seemed like reasonable, honest and relatively intelligent people. We really do need to stop making assumptions about people with no meaningful information upon which to reach an informed conclusion about them.

> **Democracy** (Greek: δημοκρατία, *dēmokratiā*, from *dēmos* 'people' and *kratos* 'rule') is a form of government in which the people have the authority to deliberate and decide legislation ("direct democracy"), or to choose governing officials to do so ("representative democracy"). Who is considered part of "the people" and how authority is shared among or delegated by the people has changed over time and at different rates in different countries, but over time more and more of a democratic country's inhabitants have generally been included. Cornerstones of democracy include freedom of assembly, association and speech, inclusiveness and equality, citizenship, consent of the governed, voting rights, freedom from unwarranted governmental

deprivation of the right to life and liberty, and minority rights.

The notion of democracy has evolved over time considerably. The original form of democracy was a direct democracy. The most common form of democracy today is a representative democracy, where the people elect government officials to govern on their behalf such as in a parliamentary or presidential democracy.[5]

The concept of representation is fine in principle, but why if I were a black Democrat would I have assumed former President Trump was going to represent my interests. Are the politicians who are introducing legislation to disenfranchise black voters in Republican states likely to represent them, when they do not even want them to be able to vote? Did Donald Trump represent the best interests of the country when he was pushing hydroxychloroquine as a cure for Covid-19 and when a man in Arizona died and his wife had to enter intensive care for ingesting this chemical? The point being that while we cannot always expect that our personal viewpoints will be

---

5   Wikipedia. *Democracy.* February 18, 2022.

represented, we should be able to expect that a politician's representation does not result in death and injuries, embarrassment for a nation, self-serving attention seeking, tantrums and the authorization of sales of weapons to kill children and create refuges in other countries. Is it representation when a child is senselessly gunned down and a politician sends "hopes and prayers", but they will not take any concrete action around gun control because politicians have received donations for their election from the National Rifle Association? I guess you could argue that it is representation but the representation is of the National Rifle Association's interests and not those of the grieving parents, who are also voters. Having a politician elected in a democracy no longer necessarily means that they will represent anyone beyond themselves and those who have funded them during their election campaign. This actually is not democracy and the United States would do better to acknowledge this and try to fix their democracy.

It should not surprise anyone that this lack of representation, when we are under the impression we are living in a democracy, does not sit well with those who need and deserve representation based on a senseless tragedy that could have been less likely to have occurred had political action been taken to curb gun violence in the past. The presumption that elected officials will automatically represent their constituents' interests is an errant assumption where the local politician represents the highest bidder, or themselves, to the exclusion of those who pay their wages. It is really quite bizarre in a way because the United States has allowed this to happen. Politicians are paid by the taxpayers who elect them to office, but then are often beholden to corporations and lobby groups who have helped them to get elected via payments of varying sizes. So, the politician's allegiances are often split between the taxpayer/voter and lobby groups and corporations. Since they will be paid by the taxpayer/voter no matter what they do, and may, or may not be paid by a corporation, or lobby group to help them get elected, they are often far more interested in ensuring that the corporations and lobby groups are happy than the electorate. Even if a politician verbally abuses their constituents, they still get paid by the taxpayers/voters who they have abused, so they can afford to disrespect these people. They would never think of abusing corporations, or lobby groups whose support is discretionary and can be stopped the moment the politician acts contrary to their interests.

Another thing that is talked about a lot in democracies is accountability. Accountability to whom?

Is it accountability to corporations and lobby groups, or accountability to the electorate? There are so many situations where it appears that politicians are catering to corporations and lobby groups that it is not even worth discussing. My motto is that if I do not understand something in politics, follow the money and power and you will never go wrong. Aside from all the rhetoric about how and why we have a moral and ethical responsibility to vote, the question is, 'why should I vote for someone to represent me, when, in reality, they will not represent me because they have been paid to represent corporations and lobby groups? Is my vote just legitimizing a system that is broken and is not democracy at all? The idea in a democracy is that each citizen is represented. If they cannot represent themselves due to huge numbers of citizens in their area, they elect someone to represent them. If this person will not do that, what is the motivation to vote? I am actually a strong advocate of voting but the problem is that there is huge money involved in politics from corporations, lobby groups, private businesses, billionaires and a host of others. When politicians should be wearing NASCAR-like jackets to show us who is filling their pockets, and why they have voted the way they have on issues, you know there is a serious problem. In the process of politicians gaining funds for election campaigns, the voter takes on increasingly less significance. There is an inverse relationship between the amount of money and number of corporations a politician receives money from and the politician's willingness and ability to represent the voter. I suppose it may all appear to be well and good until the politician finds themselves needing to represent the voters and corporations at the same time, and they have conflicting viewpoints and needs. Like when some kids get gunned down in some school but the politician has received election funding from the National Rifle Association and sends 'hopes and prayers', but does not do a damn thing of any use in trying to ensure future occurrences of these types of random shootings do not occur again. The point being that it all looks good and people may believe they are being represented until their needs conflict with those of corporations and lobby groups that have bought the politician. This is now common practice in the United States and politicians make no apology for it. You cannot have a democracy when those who are elected to represent the voter are too busy representing corporations and lobby groups to do so. This is one of the main reasons, what is left of democracy in the United States is falling apart. Big money has corrupted United States politics to a point where there are a few billionaires and corporations and lobby groups calling the shots. Being allowed to vote just creates the illusion that the voter is still being represented. It appeases the voter because, while their importance has been steadily diminishing, it allows them to maintain the illusion that they are important.

If I am a voter in the United States, and I realize that my vote means virtually nothing, I may decide not to waste my time and play the game of democracy everyone pretends exists. Why would I trust a government that puts my interests on hold while they represent corporations and lobby groups? Why does a so-called democratic government that does not represent me but, rather, represents big money, have the legitimacy to govern. Democracy is supposed to work because we are involved in the decision-making process, albeit through our representatives, that impact our daily lives. Since I am supposed to have participated in the making of the laws and rules that apply to me, I should be more willing to comply with them. Why would I feel that way when my political representative is not representing me and my opinions are irrelevant? Should I feel good about their representation when they support a factory owned by a billionaire polluting my community's drinking water while ignoring our needs as a community?

Should I feel good when a bunch of old men with grey hair ban abortion in my state so that women either need to go to another state, or seek an abortion in potentially unsafe conditions? The system continues, and so many are not actually represented in the true sense of the word, but that is okay because those in power are getting rich and that is what it is all about. It would be a joke if it were funny, but it's not, and there is not a damn thing being done about it. The motivations for many in politics actually have little to do with representation, but are far more about the acquisition of power and money. It is easy to see why, as the years have passed, politicians have been held in increasing amounts of contempt by the public. We see someone who was elected, who was a clerk, or a blue collar-worker and a few years later they are a millionaire. Yes, how did that happen? You look up the wages of Members of Parliament or the Congress and Senate and see that they make a reasonable, but not an excessively high wage, and wonder just how much they are being paid for committee work and how much they are being given by external sources to do their bidding.

Democracy needs to include trust in those who represent us. That has become increasingly difficult and particularly in the United States with all the Trump sycophants running around telling lies about the past election, about Covid-19, and anything else Trump tells them. The latest, as of the attack on the Ukraine from Trump, is that Putin is a good guy and that Republicans should support Russia attacking a sovereign country with no provocation. Yes, war crimes and attacks on countries that have done nothing to Russia are now apparently a good thing according to Trump and his sycophants. The senseless death and destruction apparently does not bother Trump or his base, which should tell everyone that Trump is not mentally well and is the last person the United States needs as a President. He is a Putin wannabe and his support for Russia and all the senseless deaths of people is a disgrace. But that is Trump. It is all about him all the time and who gets killed, or hurt does not matter to him. If it did a lot less people would have died of Covid-19 and he would have called off the attackers of the Capitol on January 6. He did not. Democracies need to be accountable to those they serve and we see time and time again politicians getting off with committing crimes that we know we would be going to jail for. The free passes given to many politicians for crimes, and the Presidential pardons dished out by Trump made a mockery of the entire United States justice system. Some white financial manager steals millions from investors and gets a slap on the wrist and a black man caught with a few grams of cocaine goes to jail for years. The point being that legitimacy requires fairness and the appearances of fairness and justice. Everyone knows that there is a justice system for wealthy whites and one for everyone else in North America. Legitimacy to govern also involves adherence to the Constitution in terms of equality and fairness. These are things that were given little respect by former President Trump and his unqualified staff, who were hired through nepotism and prior relationships, rather than qualifications and competence.

The legitimacy to govern involves meeting standards of ethical and behavioural conduct. It includes respect and protection of the Constitution and representing all constituents concerns equally and putting them on at minimum an equal playing field with corporations and lobby groups. It involves acting in the best interests of the electorate even when doing so may not necessarily be in the best interests of the politician. I think politicians that are sincere must be prepared to resign and be willing to vote to protect the Constitution and the best interests of the country, even if doing so may hurt their chances of re-election. The problem we see today is that the interests of politicians, particularly in the United States supersede all else. It is this selfish, all about me attitude that is killing democracy and the United States, as politicians repeatedly put themselves before the oath they took to protect their Constitution and their country. There are all kinds of Republican politicians at all levels of government supporting the Big Lie about Trump winning the 2020 election when they all know this is not true. Yet, they do this because they believe that attaching themselves to Trump's lies, conspiracy theories and corruption will bode well for their political careers. They know it will harm the country but could apparently care less. The problem being that the next generation is facing enough problems now without having them thrown into a totalitarian society, along with combating all the natural disasters caused by global warming that cause massive damage, famine, even greater poverty and likely violence as people become increasingly desperate. But people like Trump and the Koch's never have enough, no matter how much wealth they have. Trump took great delight in sticking it to the poor through excessive taxation that fills the pockets of the wealthy. Then after the rich were given a massive tax break Mitch McConnell said that social security and the food stamp program would need to be cut to pay down the deficit but that the two were not related.

What happened was that the deficit was increased to pay the wealthy when the United States did not have the money. Then they wanted to cut essential programs for the poor to pay for their unmitigated greed. The problem here is that the same class of people who Trump's class of people exploit can hardly wait to vote for him so he can further exploit them. And everyone is supposed to pretend democracy is working and live what is left of the American Dream. It is quickly changing from a dream into a nightmare but like all the lies and conspiracy theories people are still supposed to believe in the fantasy of the American Dream, that is nothing more than a fantasy designed to excuse the greed of the rich and blame the working poor and homeless for their lot in life. It is the worst sort of emotional abuse and does not excuse a few percent of the population having close to 90+% of the wealth. It is never enough and the ultra-wealthy will likely not be happy until they have 99% of the wealth and the rest of the population must subsist on 1% and supposedly live the American Dream.

The idea that politicians can keep attacking the poor and middle class to give to those who have plenty already is flawed economics. This is because you could have $10 billion and what does it matter when the poor have finally had enough abuse and rise up against those who have abused them. When this happens, the poor will be blamed for the insurrection when in fact they will have little choice if they want to enjoy any semblance of a decent life. It will not be the poor who should be blamed but the politicians who keep taking from them to keep their rich cronies and election campaigns supporting corporations happy. There will soon be a tipping point reached and things are going to get very ugly as conflicting agendas confront each other. The right will be interested in protecting white privilege and the left will be interested in ensuring their survival through a more equitable distribution of resources. Anyone can see that the ever-increasing demand that fuels a capitalist economy cannot continue forever, and especially when the poor and middle class have increasingly less to spend, and particularly on discretionary items. But the politicians continue to live in fantasies, conspiracy theories and lies that are commonly accepted by the public. To have the legitimacy to govern one must deal with reality and promote equality in all aspects of life. Isn't that the essence of the Constitution? The Constitution is not a document that should be applied when it is convenient and politically expedient but ignored when it is not.

Even personal integrity is so lacking in politics it is pathetic. We see people like Ted Cruz, Mitch

McConnell and Josh Hawley change their stances on issues almost as frequently as babies need their diapers changed. It is all about what is politically expedient at the moment. It is not about having morals, ethics and values that inform decision-making but rather polls, appeasing Donald Trump and being like an amoeba that has no spine. It is ridiculous to expect that a bunch of people with no integrity will gain the legitimacy to govern, in the same way we don't bring a bunch of criminals together to figure out how to create a more honest society. As they say in many self-help groups, "if you don't possess it, you cannot give it a way." If you lack integrity, ethics, morals and values beyond serving oneself you are incapable of bringing legitimacy to the political process and best stay out of it. Of course, while these people may lack integrity and other desirable characteristics, they do not lack a lust for power and money. There are some Republican politicians that possess the integrity needed to govern, although their mere participation in the political process with its inherent requirement to gain money to get elected brings their integrity into question. Do the ends really justify the means? I suppose if one does not play the game they will not be elected and cannot make some positive changes. So, the individual may have integrity but must enter a cesspool of corruption to instigate positive change, if they are able to do so. It is like having to use banned substances to compete in some Olympic sports. There are a few Republican politicians I respect and none support Donald Trump, the lies, conspiracy theories, fiction about January 6 and all the other garbage the party under Trump has become known for. How can you have the legitimacy to govern when you refuse to deal with reality, or are running around to white supremacist events when many of your constituents are people of colour. This is precisely what Taylor-Green and Gosar did recently. It is ironic that Trump has done many things that support white supremacy but where are the Republicans when he attacks people of colour, or treats people of colour as if they were third class citizens when compared to how he treats whites on the same issues. Why is Trump not reigning in Taylor-Greene and Gosar if he is not a white supremacist?

> WASHINGTON — GOP leaders in the House and the Senate on Monday denounced a pair of far-right Trump allies — Reps. Marjorie Taylor Greene, R-Ga., and Paul Gosar, R-Ariz. — for speaking at a gathering of white nationalists in Florida over the weekend.

"There's no place in the Republican Party for white supremacists or antisemitism," Senate Minority Leader Mitch McConnell, R-Ky., said in a terse statement.

House Minority Leader Kevin McCarthy, R-Calif., told reporters for CNN and Punchbowl News that it was "appalling and wrong" for the two lawmakers to attend the meeting in Florida and that he plans to discuss the matter with them.

"There's no place in our party for any of this. ... The party should not be associated any time, any place with somebody who is antisemitic," said McCarthy, who recently returned from leading a delegation of House Republicans to Israel. "This is unacceptable."[6]

It seems when Donald Trump has done things and said things that are clearly racist there is often silence in the Republican party and this is because polls show the party is largely racist. The same is true of the white evangelicals that tend to support the party in

---

6   Scott Wong. NBC News. *GOP leaders denounce Greene, Gosar for speaking at white nationalist event.* February 28, 2022.

great numbers. Wasn't it ironic how these people have come out to speak against Taylor-Greene's and Gosar's involvement at a white supremacist event but have nothing to say about all the Republican states bringing in legislation to disenfranchise voters of colour? I didn't hear any Republicans take specific exception to the Oath Keepers and Proud Boys being involved in the attack on the Capitol January 6 and they are clearly white supremacist groups. So, it is difficult to take the comments of the Republicans who oppose their colleagues participation in a white supremacist event seriously. Only Mitt Romney, of the Republican party stayed and clapped when the first black woman was appointed to the United States Supreme Court, when traditionally almost all politicians have stayed and clapped as a show of respect to the appointee, regardless of their political affiliation. The Republican party is predominantly racist and Trump's base is also, so it is a fine line to tread when one wishes to address racism in a party that largely supports it.

> The rare criticism of fellow Republican lawmakers by GOP leaders, which followed fierce condemnation of Greene and Gosar from Republicans across the political spectrum, highlighted how the two represent a major political liability for the party as it

seeks to win back control of the House and the Senate this fall.

Sen. Mitt Romney, R-Utah, called Greene and Gosar "morons" in an appearance on CNN, while Rep. Liz Cheney, R-Wyo., said her House colleagues are promoting anti-semitism and white supremacy that is "a toxin in the bloodstream."

Even some high-profile Trump allies said they were disgusted. Former Secretary of State Mike Pompeo tweeted that Greene was "playing footsie" with "anti-Semitic neo-Nazis." And Rep. Jim Banks, R-Ind., the head of the conservative Republican Study Committee, also did not mince words.

"It's unbecoming for a member of Congress to speak at an event that's promoted by anyone who espouses those views," Banks told NBC News. "This is an event that no Republican should attend ... and it's unfortunate that she did."[7]

---

7   Scott Wong. NBC News. *GOP leaders denounce Greene, Gosar for speaking at white nationalist event.* February 28, 2022.

Mike Pompeo was in the Trump administration and I do not recall him coming out and saying that the election was not stolen, or that he opposed Trump's racist comments and behaviour. It is ironic that he should mention neo-Nazis when his own party has no use for democracy at this point, and Trump would clearly like to be a dictator as evidenced by the attempted coup of January 6. I suspect the truth is that Gosar and Taylor-Greene hold the same values as many Republican politicians but unlike most, express their racist views in public rather than behind the scenes. The good news is that these two politicians along with politicians like Hawley, Jordan and Boebert do a great deal to hurt the party with their hateful and divisive comments. Those doing the work of running the country and making positive contributions to the national politics in the United States don't have time for this stupidity. These two may have just alienated thousands of voters of colour through their selfishness and stupidity. The potential Republican voters are confronted with which Republican party to vote for. The extreme-right, represented in part by Taylor-Greene, or the one represented by more moderates like Hogan and Mitt Romney.

Controversy is nothing new for Greene and Gosar. Both were involved in an effort last year to launch an "America First Caucus" to protect "Anglo-Saxon political traditions"; the idea was dropped after members of both parties panned it.

A year ago this month, all House Democrats — along with 11 Republicans — voted to boot Greene off her two committees after it was revealed that her past Facebook posts espoused antisemitic conspiracy theories and violence against Democratic politicians.

And in November, all House Democrats and two Republicans voted to censure Gosar and remove him from his committees after he tweeted an anime video depicting him killing Rep. Alexandria Ocasio-Cortez, D-N.Y.

In the latter two instances, Democrats forced floor votes after McCarthy refused to take disciplinary action against Greene and Gosar. McCarthy has said he would put Gosar and Greene back on their committees if Republicans win the House in the midterm elections.[8]

---

8   Scott Wong. NBC News. *GOP leaders denounce Greene, Gosar for speaking at a white nationalisy even.* February 28, 2022.

Kevin McCarthy is another politician in the Republican party that is a Trump sycophant. The fact he would not take action against two party members who were speaking at a white supremacist event tells you all you need to know about him. Not only that but he plans to reinstate them on Committees they were removed from due to their behaviour, if the Republicans win the House in the midterm elections. It would appear that McCarthy supports their speaking at a white supremacist event and actually wishes to reward them in spite of his comments to the contrary. Since McCarthy lacks a spine and is essentially little more than a mouthpiece for Donald Trump, it is safe to assume that Trump also supports the actions of these two individuals. He certainly did not condemn their racist actions. Should people of colour see the Republican party as having the legitimacy to govern when the party as a whole does not see them as equal citizens, or as having an equal right to vote? Yes, I know, what about the Constitution? It seems to be of little interest to many Republicans. It is a good thing when it fits what they are doing and is to be ignored when it is not.

Wars and Natural Disasters

There are times in every country when it is necessary that people put their differences aside and work collectively toward the common good. Times of major crises are like this. We see neighbours helping each other and providing emotional support to each other after a tornado has destroyed many homes in a community. We see the same on the east coast of the United States when major flooding and damage results from a hurricane. One day life is great and the next a person is left looking at what were once their home and car. When disasters strike, or have been predicted to strike, people look to their governments for support for everything from manpower, to sandbags, to cleaning up debris, to providing shelter for those who no longer have any. It is during these times that we hear of incredible kindness and sacrifice for the benefit of others. These stories provide hope that we can still respond as a community when the situation warrants it. Collective needs require collective responses and these types of responses are far more effective than acting as a group of uncoordinated individuals.

On a broader scale this is also true when we saw Trump alienate allies and question why NATO existed. If the United States were responding to the war in Ukraine alone the impact would be far less significant than when a united NATO, and other non-NATO countries join forces and respond to the attack on the Ukraine by Russia, *en masse* in a coordinated manner. Whether it be trying to deal with crime in a neighbourhood, or bringing a dictator under control, collective responses are critically important when dealing with some issues. We expect various levels of government to coordinate these collective efforts and to each do their part. This makes sense because in democratic societies we assume that those we elect will represent us and the collective needs of the people who reside in a place struck by a natural disaster. While it makes sense to assume this, it is not always the case. Some politicians, like Rand Paul for example, would not support any requests for Federal aid for communities hit by natural disasters. That is until his home state of Kentucky was hit by a tornado and then he began begging for the aid that he had apparently been so happy to try to deny other states and communities hit by equally devastating storms. In other words, I don't want to help you, but when I need help you should help me. Obviously, this type of thinking will not work very well as we face more and more severe weather as the planet warms. Politicians who are all about meeting their own needs are obviously a major liability as we move into far more challenging times.

Dealing with natural disasters may seem unrelated to the legitimacy to govern but it is not. If politicians cannot act in a nonpartisan way to support Americans, or Canadians when there is a natural disaster, they should not be in office. The major rift we see in the United States makes me wonder if any major problem the country has to confront will be magnified many-fold due to the unwillingness of politicians to cooperate for the benefit of Americans. We see it with Mitch McConnell blocking bills that will help Americans and we see it when politicians come out and say that they will not support any legislation proposed by the opposing party, no matter how good it may be. It is this type of selfish garbage that made Covid-19 so much worse in the United States than it needs to have been. Partisan politics resulted in hundreds, if not thousands of unnecessary deaths because public health measures were politicized by Donald Trump and the Republican party. Trump continued to hold rallies that were super spreader events and many Republicans chose not to get vaccinated, or wear masks to show support for Donald Trump, in spite of him getting vaccinated. It showed that to some, politics were far more important to them than the lives of those who were paying them to be represented. The chasm in the United States makes me wonder if Americans would even pull together if there was a war, horrific famine, massive earthquake, or repeated storms that decimated communities. Perhaps this is where we need to ask ourselves why neighbours help each other but many of the political bodies representing Americans refuse to work together. Who is being represented when the public wants assistance, and is doing one thing, and the politicians are doing quite another? Who for example, was Donald Trump representing as people were dropping like flies from Covid-19 and he went off on stupid rants about hydro chloroquine and UV light curing Covid-19, when in fact they don't?

We all make errors in our jobs and so do politicians. It is one thing to make an honest mistake and quite another to make a deliberate malicious mistake that causes suffering and death. Those people who act out of self-interest when doing so causes suffering and deaths among those who pay for their representation, do not have the legitimacy to govern. Nor do people like Donald Trump who held super spreader events knowing full well that those who attended his rallies without masks, social distancing, or vaccinations were likely to contract the virus and could die. He took an oath to protect and help the American people, yet seemed to have cared less how many died because it was all part of the process of the narcissist realizing his goal. The deaths of others and the suffering of those who lost loved ones was immaterial to Trump as his goals superseded any concerns about the health and welfare of the American people. Donald Trump has no place in a democracy because he is all about Donald Trump and only Donald Trump. Only when his needs and desires align with the needs of America do we see him represent America's best interests. One only needs to look at his support for Russia's attack on Ukraine. The rest of the western world is placing sanctions on Russia for this totally unwarranted attack. But Donald Trump apparently has strong ties with Russia and according to some shows I have watched, his businesses were bailed out with Russian money, so unlike 99% of the people in the west, Trump supported the attack by Russia on Ukraine. Has he been bought and paid for by powers in Russia? I will leave you to draw your own conclusions. The world can no longer afford to have people like Donald Trump in power because the building of local and global collectives is critical to being able to respond to increasing challenges. The days of chest beating and telling anyone who will listen that "we can go it alone" are over. Those who do not wish to participate in collective efforts will perish.

I imagine Russia is feeling very alone at this point. It has gone it alone in attacking Ukraine, and due to being a dictatorship has failed to foster relationships with potential allies. Few countries will join Russia in responding collectively to the international sanctions placed on Russia or, opposing the actions of NATO. When you have the weight of global sanctions impacting your economy, you have a disaster on your hands. Especially if you needn't expect to receive any help from your friends in addressing the sanctions facing you. It can be a lonely world when countries and individuals like Russia and Trump want to play bully and go it alone. It is reasonable to think that the vast majority of the world would like to see the bullies get what they have coming to them after the unprovoked attack on Ukraine and Donald Trump's insulting remarks directed toward other world leaders, and pulling the U.S. out of many global bodies that were formed to address global issues.

Canada has been quite good in this regard and when there is a problem in Canada, or elsewhere in the world Canada has risen to the occasion most times, although the evacuation of Afghanistan citizens who had aided Canada, certainly left something to be desired. I think Canada is well positioned, and in fact better positioned than the Americans to deal with the massive problems that may lay ahead. I don't say this because Canada has huge military strength like the United States, or a large population, but rather because with socialist programs like the Canadian Pension Plan and Universal Health Care we have been taught to think more in terms of we than United States citizens where the emphasis is placed on individual rights before all else. This is not to say that the United States is not doing its part because Joe Biden has helped to bring NATO allies together again. It is to say that at an individual and community level it may be easier for Canadians to accept that we must work collectively to tackle huge issues like global warming and natural disasters. We have been trained to think this way, whereas in the United States there is nothing more sacred than individual rights. To see that this is true all one needs to do is to look at the two different countries approaches to gun violence and gun control. In Canada, it is fair to say that collective safety overrides the right of the individual to own a gun, whereas in the United States it does not. This is not a knock on the United States but may make pulling together to respond collectively in the United States much more difficult.

I am not saying that neighbours do not help one another, but we see legislation being blocked that would help all U.S. citizens because of partisanship. We see Trump and other Republicans come out in support of Putin and Russia. This is not at all consistent with the official United States position. It just creates problems for the United States government to stay engaged in the NATO response to the war in Ukraine because many Republicans are supporting and promoting the criminal actions of a dictator.

If, as has been suggested in many programs and articles, Trump was bailed out by some entity in Russia when his financial empire was about to collapse, surely, he would then be in a conflict of interest if he were elected president in 2024. This is because his personal views and statements differ from those of the United States government. Donald Trump always does what is best for Donald Trump and I suspect that is why he supposedly changed his tune in regard to the invasion of Ukraine. Few Americans support the invasion and those that do are on the fringes, so Trump did himself no favours by coming out in support of

Russia and its dictator Vladimir Putin. Trump cozied up to Putin throughout his whole presidency. Then there were the private meetings with Putin where Trump destroyed the translator's notes immediately after these meetings. I don't believe for a minute that Donald Trump does not support Putin, or the Russian attack on Ukraine. What I do believe is that Trump saw that his comments about supporting the attack were highly unpopular, so he changed his story, but not his actual thoughts.

> ORLANDO, Fla., Feb 26 (Reuters) – Former President Donald Trump condemned on Saturday Russia's invasion of Ukraine and said he was praying for Ukrainians, switching tone from his praise for Russian President Vladimir Putin earlier this week. Trump's remarks at the CPAC conservative gathering in Florida came hours after the United States and allies announced sweeping new sanctions that would kick some Russian banks off the main global payments systems and limit the ability of Russia's central bank to support the rouble. Addressing an adoring crowd at an event that touts itself as the world's largest conservative gathering, Trump used his speech to bash

Democratic President Joe Biden and again hint at a possible run for president in 2024. Trump had irked some Republican party members by describing Putin's actions in Ukraine, where cities have been pounded by Russian artillery and cruise missiles, as "genius" and "pretty savvy."[9]

Of course, Fox mouthpiece Tucker Carlson who speaks publicly on behalf of the Republican party seems to be in favour of the invasion of Ukraine by Russia, even if it is a violation of international law and an investigation is being undertaken to see if war crimes have been committed by Russia. The Republicans and Fox News never seem to let the facts get in the way of a good story. The Republican party under Trump presently rejects democracy because the party also supports maintaining white privilege at any cost. With growing numbers of non-white voters, democracy in the United States will result in less white power and greater power enjoyed by those of colour. To people like Trump and Carlson this cannot be allowed to happen, so they parade out their hate and racism at every opportunity.

---

9   Alexandra Ulmar. Reuters. *Trump condemns Russia invasion; hints again at 2024 presidential run.* February 27, 2022.

People across the left — including me — routinely lambaste Fox News megastar Tucker Carlson for his alarming right-wing populist screeds. But this past week, as Carlson downplayed concerns about Russia's invasion of Ukraine up until Moscow began a full-fledged incursion, something striking happened: Critics began to deem him a "traitor."

For some activists, lawmakers and commentators, Carlson's decision to minimize Russia's imminent invasion and push back against critics of Russian President Vladimir Putin meant he was siding with Russia against the U.S. But that's a misread. Carlson isn't in favour of Russia over America or angling to aid Russia in dominating or controlling the U.S. — he wants the U.S. to *be like Russia*. And in accordance with paleoconservative and white nationalist principles, he has an aversion to foreign interventionism so American militarism can grow at home. Carlson's ideas are dangerous and must be fought, but loyalty rhetoric misses the real problem. Furthermore, the traitor insult is one that could derail the quality of our national debate at a critical time. Setting Carlson aside, there is great risk in associating opposition to war with betrayal of the republic.[10]

Tucker Carlson is like Trump in that he will do anything for attention and to increase Fox ratings. Like Trump, Carlson cares about himself and apparently does not care if he does damage to the United States through the spread of misinformation, hatred, racism and his desire for the United States to emulate Russia. In spite of this, Trump supporters in particular tune in to his program and listen to his misinformation, nonsense and garbage, perhaps thinking they are actually listening to the news.

> In the run-up to the invasion, Carlson persistently downplayed the severity of what Russia could be doing and pushed back against the prospect of American involvement. He characterized the situation as a "border dispute," distracting from the reality of Russia's yearlong meddling in eastern Ukraine and the illegality of Putin's recognizing and ordering troops into Ukraine's

---

10   Zeeshan Aleen. MSNBC. *The real reason Tucker Carlson supports Russia's Putin.* February 28, 2022.

eastern separatist-held regions. Carlson argued Ukraine was "not a democracy" to denigrate the case for America's supporting it. He posited a ludicrous theory that Democrats stand to benefit financially from war in Ukraine. And he delivered a long monologue about how Americans are socialized to hate Putin even though he's not responsible for what Carlson sees as Americans' primary social ills ("Has Putin ever called me a racist? Has he threatened to get me fired for disagreeing with him? Has he shipped every middle-class job in my town to Russia?"). That monologue was, in fact, replayed by Russian state-sponsored television because it served naturally as Russian propaganda.[11]

When you hear that the Russian government is playing clips of Tucker Carlson on its public airwaves to promote that it is doing nothing wrong in Ukraine, you know there is a serious problem. Yet, it continues unabated, or until someone tells Carlson to shut up, or to change his tune. It is a shame when the media will

---

11   Zeeshan Aleen. MSNBC. *The real reason Tucker Carlson supports Russia's Putin*. February 28, 2022.

deliberately try to create divisions when the country needs a united front. Interestingly, NATO and many other countries that are not NATO members were levying sanctions against Russia as Carlson and, previously Trump, tried to justify the totally unwarranted and illegal attack on Ukraine.

> Carlson and his ideological allies, like Steve Bannon and Donald Trump, see in Putin someone with a shared worldview — authoritarian, fiercely nationalistic, happily bigoted.[12]

Americans had better figure out if they want a supposedly federal democratic state with Trump as its dictator, just as Russia is with Putin, or if the country wishes to maintain its democracy. This is because the country is perilously close to becoming a dictatorship and most Republican states are making this increasingly likely through employing partisan hacks to work in elections, through the disenfranchisement of voters of colour and through things like gerrymandering. The question is whether the Federal Government with Manchin, acting as a Republican, can pass an election act that ensures that elections are legal and fair. If not,

---

12   Zeeshan Aleen. MSNBC. *The real reason Tucker Carlson supports Russia's Putin*. February 28, 2022.

one must wonder if President Biden will do this via executive orders, or if the Supreme Court will render decisions that move the country closer to a right-wing dictatorship, or back to a democracy. I have little confidence in the Supreme Court at this point.

The varied and at times conflicting Republican reactions, both on the campaign trail and on Capitol Hill, underscore how the party remains deeply influenced by Trump, who praised Vladimir Putin as "savvy" after the Russian president recognized the independence of two Russian separatist-controlled areas in Eastern Ukraine. As Russia began its full-scale invasion later Wednesday, Trump told Fox News that "This all happened because of a rigged election." At a Mar-a-Lago fundraiser Wednesday evening, he continued his praise of Putin, calling him "pretty smart" in "taking over a country for $2 worth of sanctions." (Video of the remarks was circulated on Twitter by American Bridge, a national Democratic super PAC.) While most Republicans have baulked at Putin's moves in Ukraine and called for swift and steep sanctions, others aligned with Trump have echoed the former president and adopted a far less hostile view of the Russian leader and been more circumspect about any U.S. military action in Europe. That sentiment has been bolstered by Trump allies on prominent media platforms, many of whom have been framing Washington's alarm about Russia as an establishment, even elitist, concern.[13]

The critical question is whether, or not, with political and media forces that wish to scrap democracy in the United States, if it can survive. Does Donald Trump have the legitimacy to govern if elected, if he is in bed with the Russians and he must make critical decisions around the conflict between Russia and Ukraine? Yes, he could be legally elected and in the strictest sense have the legitimacy to govern but there is an obvious, massive conflict of interest. If Trump wins the election and the war continues will the United States honour its NATO commitments?

If the Constitution talks about equality and freedom under the law, shouldn't those politicians who wish to remove the freedoms of the United States citizenry be held to account for their breaches of the

---

13 Caitlin Huey-Burns, Robert Costa. CBS News. *Trump's response to Putin's invasion of Ukraine reveals divisions among Republicans.* January 25, 2022.

oath of office they took to defend the Constitution. Or, is it okay to pay lip service to the Constitution and support measures like disenfranchising black voters, the elderly, disabled and others that may be more likely to vote Democrat? When put to the test are there to be any reprisals for violating the Constitution if you are a member of the House or Senate? Or is the Constitution like the American Dream, in that everyone refers to it, but the reality is it is largely ceremonial, or is a document that can largely be ignored, but referred to when it is self-serving, or politically expedient to do so? If, when we elect people, and they take an oath of office, is it not reasonable to expect that politicians act in accordance with this oath?

None of the things that we used to think were sacred seem to be any more. when these things that are so critical to having a decent, pleasant life are destroyed there is no consequence for those who are doing it. The problem is that when you write policy, you write it to curb potential abuses that may occur. If you were writing policy for the House, Senate and President of the United States to create parameters around what can be done and not done, you may assume the people in these positions would be honourable and you may errantly assume that certain rules would not be necessary. Donald Trump took full advantage of these serious oversights. These policies and rules were written for honourable people and not the Donald Trumps of the world. That is why Donald Trump was able to get away with his lying, racism and a huge number of other abuses. For example, there is no policy that states that if anyone dies as a result of your lies you will be held to account. Or if you want to spread misinformation and hold super spreader events, you will be held responsible for all the medical costs and deaths that ensue. No, you just walk away because the people who created the policies likely thought that an honourable person would not tell lies that would kill people, or hold maskless events that resulted in many becoming ill and some dying. No one anticipated such a dishonest, corrupt and morally bankrupt person could become president but they did, and the damage has been immense.

There is freedom of speech in the United States but you will notice that there is not a requirement that it is accompanied by responsibility. I suspect when the idea of freedom of speech first surfaced and seemed like a good idea, no one envisioned the United States media undermining the United States and saying things that another country has replayed as part of their propaganda campaign to appease their population, after initiating a senseless war. Tucker Carlson always seeks greater ratings and money and his behaviour and the impact of it seem to be of little concern to him.

> MOSCOW (The Borowitz Report)—After placing strict bans on journalists' coverage of Russia's war against Ukraine, Vladimir Putin clarified that any ban on journalists did not include Tucker Carlson. "When it was reported that I was limiting the reporting of journalists, some may have misconstrued that to include Tucker," Putin said. "To the contrary, I am an enormous fan of his work and want him to continue doing what he's doing." "It pains me to think that I might have unintentionally insulted Tucker Carlson," he said. "His work has given me great joy." Putin said that he was issuing his clarification out of an abundance of caution. "I had thought that it was clear that I didn't mean Tucker Carlson when I said 'journalists,'" he said.[14]

No doubt, Putin is an enormous fan of Carlson's work when Russia has been playing clips of him to excuse Russia's senseless attack on Ukraine to the Russian people. This is a disgrace and should embarrass

---

14   Andy Borowitz. The New Yorker. *Tucker Carlson*. March 3, 2022.

every United States citizen even if Tucker Carlson is a Trump sycophant who will say and do anything for money and attention. A morally and ethically bankrupt person who stands for nothing other than himself and his wants and desires. It is little wonder Carlson, Trump and Putin get along so well. While Trump was talking about how savvy and smart Putin was, Carlson, like a good little lap dog, was spreading views that were consistent with Trump's. Of course, Trump is Putin's lap dog and there is no question that Trump has ties to Russia. People can argue that Trump's love of Russia and Putin is not a reason why he would not have the legitimacy to govern if he were to win the 2024 presidential election. There is truth to this because the public has a responsibility to inform themselves, and if they wish to elect a man who wishes to emulate Putin, they have the legal right to do so. They also have the right to put up with another four years of Trump trying to undermine NATO, kissing Putin's behind and general incompetence while Trump engages in transactional relations that benefit him personally.

If people like Donald Trump and Tucker Carlson think so much of Russia one can only wish that they would move there permanently. If they think that a dictatorship is a superior form of governance to democracy there are many places they may find more desirable than the United States, like China and North Korea for example. Of course, they will not move because in spite of their white nationalism, complaints and whining they have become rich within this horrible democratic society called the United States. The problem they see with democracy has to do with losing white privilege and I suppose they may feel that things like ethnic cleansing may be easier in a communist, or fascist country. They have had every advantage being white males but it is not enough. Just because they have become rich does not mean they would not happily deny people of colour the right to vote, or to have a reasonable standard of living. To them the United States should be a white country and people of colour are going to increasingly diminish white privilege as their numbers increase. This is the issue underlying most of the United States present problems and explains why many in the Republican party are now wanting a form of government other than democracy.

A dictatorship may be considered legitimate by a small group of privileged elites like we see in Russia with the oligarchs. In communist countries we sometimes see governments that appear to have the legitimacy to govern but, do they, if they jail opponents, persecute minorities, kill journalists and have judges who render decisions they do not like killed?

This does not automatically mean that communist governments lack legitimacy. If they adhere to international law and act in what they perceive as the best interests of their population they may be seen to have legitimacy. In any country there are actions taken by governments that are more widely supported than others. With a country like China, millions of people have been helped to escape poverty by the communist government. There are, and have been allegations of major human rights abuses and so, as it is with any country, there is a balance between positive and negative aspects of a country's governance. It is difficult to assess the degree of legitimacy a government like the Chinese one has because I am aware that I am regularly bombarded with negative propaganda about China that did not fit my experience when I visited there, or with the people I know from China. One may argue the legitimacy to govern is irrelevant because we all are governed whether our governments are legitimate, or illegitimate.

In the United States the politicians cannot even agree on whether the January 6 insurrection was a normal tourist visit or an illegal coup to overthrow an elected democratic government. Partisan politics should have no place when addressing national security threats and natural disasters but the Republicans seem to want to politicize everything from wearing masks to combat Covid-19 to people's rights to vote. This makes the United States highly vulnerable and, if politicians continue to refuse to work in a bipartisan way these problems have the potential to end life in the country as we know it. Politicians need to ask themselves what good their partisan politics will do if the country is decimated by natural disasters and there is no cohesive effort to address the fallout. It is with incredible selfishness that many act, and those particularly who have aligned themselves with Donald Trump. All the gains through selfishness and greed will mean little if much of the country is uninhabitable for some reason. It is highly frustrating watching politicians put themselves before all else when they are at a tipping point and there is a critical need for a collective political voice to lead through the tough times ahead.

Insight,
or Lack Thereof

When I used to listen to politicians like Hawley, Trump, Cruz, Boebert, Taylor-Green and Gosar, I used to wonder if they were stupid, or just self-centered people with little backbone, and little to offer the country they are being paid to serve. Certainly, some are clearly not very bright and others are reasonably intelligent but are extremely self-centered and greedy. Donald Trump is the poster boy for selfishness and greed so it should come as no surprise that his sycophants emulate this unpleasant quality. Rather than wondering how they can better represent the people who elected them, and pay them, they seem far more interested in what is in it for them. Can they gain monetarily, or in terms of the power they possess? It is all about them and the Constitution and country are apparently a secondary consideration. When I watch some of these politicians, I am reminded of public schools where some kids focus on their needs to the exclusion of the needs of others. Some politicians appear to be operating at this juvenile level.

The question I find myself asking is whether these people have no insight, or if they are fully cognizant of what their actions are doing to their country and they simply don't care? It is sad when constituencies feel that people like McCarthy, Boebert, Manchin, and Taylor-Green can do a good job of representing their interests. With people like this in positions of power it makes me wonder what will happen when the country encounters major problems that require political leadership. People who are good at increasing divisions amongst people but who lack the skills and backbone necessary to pull the country together and help people unite to deal with a major problem, like famine, war, or global warming.

When politicians wish to promote some alternate reality like the Big Lie that Trump won the election he lost to Biden, you know the United States has a serious problem. If the vast majority of Republicans do not want democracy and are promoting lies, misinformation and conspiracy theories one has to ask what chance the country has of dealing with real problems that are not explained away through some far-fetched nonsensical conspiracy theory. Even if politicians are unaware of how their rhetoric is hurting democracy in the United States, they are aware of the oath they took to defend the Constitution. Insurrections and coups to overthrow the government are not supported by the Constitution and nor is the desire by many Republicans to throw out democracy and give Trump what he has always wanted; a dictatorship. The politicians who cozy up to Trump for his endorsements know full well that they are hurting democracy. They know that Trump was involved in the coup of January 6 where people were calling for the death of Vice President Pence. This all occurred while Trump sat in the White House watching the insurrection on television. He would not call off the attack on the Capitol, or try to put an end to the violence. Donald Trump showed no leadership in this situation, just like he never does when assuming a leadership role does not directly benefit him. It is actually quite remarkable that a man so self-centred could be elected to represent approximately 330 million people, when the only person he has any interest in representing is himself.

In a democracy a leader must possess the desire to help others. That is the crux of the job of the politician. We all expect to get paid when we work but tend to enter professions because we possess specific qualities and interests. Social workers, nurses and doctors tend to be people who would like to help others. Police and people in the military are generally interested in law and order and see the value in structure and a society that is not characterized by anarchy. In the same way those who enter religious occupations and politics should be people who wish to help others through their jobs. Unfortunately, as we all know, some people, who may have been initially well-intentioned end up doing more harm than good; the paedophile priest, the social worker who steals funds, the politician who promotes racism, division and hate. We generally think that these people represent a small minority, but do they? In the Republican party we saw about 90% who voted against impeaching President Trump, the vast majority promote the Big Lie with no hesitation and, many have come out with homophobic, racist and misogynistic tweets. So, while we might think that there are a few bad politicians, the reality is that the vast majority of Republicans have voted in ways that have harmed democracy and served to destroy their own country in many different ways. One of the biggest things they have done is to create and then foster major divisions in the country that may result in civil war in the near future. These politicians refer to the United States as the greatest country on the planet and speak about the benefits of freedom and democracy, but there are those, including former President Trump who have made statements supporting the atrocities in Ukraine. If according to many Republicans, the United States is the best country on the planet, and they like freedom and democracy, why are they doing everything they possibly can to destroy it? Either they are lying when they say they like freedom and democracy, or they are not intelligent enough to see how democracy is being incrementally destroyed by them and their colleagues. I suspect it is the former. Fox News is only too happy to have employees that support the Russian attacks on Ukraine and spread seeds of doubt about the illegitimacy of the attacks by Russia, in the same way they spread misinformation about the validity of the last election that Joe Biden won.

So, the people getting paid to represent their constituents like Republican mouthpiece Marjorie Taylor-Greene make racist statements and do immense harm, but Republican Kevin McCarthy, Minority Leader of the United States House of Representatives refuses to reign her in, making him complicit in her ongoing attacks on democracy, minorities and those who do not see the world as she does. This is because McCarthy desperately wants to retain his position and by attacking Taylor-Greene he may upset Trump and his base. So instead of having a backbone and stating what he believes, he changes his tune frequently and lets political expediency be his guide, rather than any solid set of values, morals or ethics. He is a power-hungry amoeba. He actually personifies the Trump party because the party has no platform, no ideas and supports whatever Donald Trump thinks it should do. Following a man who is a narcissist is likely not the best course of action because a major part of narcissism is chronic self-centredness to the exclusion of all else, including other people. Not a good fit in a democracy where the job is all about representing others and not one's own selfish interests. It requires the ability to persuade and garner support for ideas.

For many, politics in the United States is all about money and many people enter politics as members of the middle class and then dramatically increase their wealth. Funny how that works when the base salaries do not align well with the amount of wealth these people quickly accumulate. So, what we refer to as democracy in the United States is as much of a conspiracy theory as anything else. Real democracy is not all about how can I fill my pockets if I am elected and how can I climb into bed with corporations and lobby groups that will give me money that will make my pay as a politician comparatively look like chump change. Nothing will change because politicians are not about to bite the hand that feeds them. Doing so would make their actions consistent with defending the United States Constitution and supporting democracy, rather than this perverse so-called version of it that is driven by money virtually to the exclusion of all else.

If it is true that power corrupts it should follow, that like the President, all politicians can only hold office for two terms. This would likely make for less corruption and would also make for far better decision-making when politicians do not have to worry about being re-elected after their second terms. Those who are corrupt have no legitimacy to govern and it is not particularly helpful to have people in their seventies and eighties in political positions when they should have been long retired. We need an injection of new ideas and ways of thinking to tackle many of the new problems we face. In the same way that elders in many cultures have trouble understanding young people within their cultures, eighty-year-olds are seldom as knowledgeable about social media, computer hacking, espionage and a host of other major recent technological advances as younger people. This is not to minimize the value of seniors but is simply to say that some need to move on so that young people who want to deal with issues like climate change, alternative energy, social media issues and a host of other things have the opportunity to do so. I wish the days of 70–80-year-old grey haired men sitting around a table discussing what should be done about women's reproductive rights were over and the men were replaced by young women who this issue directly impacts. Ironically, some man gets elected and all of a sudden sees himself as an authority on women's reproductive health and feels that he should be afforded major input and decision-making power on the issue. It is bizarre. In any other field one is expected to be qualified to become an expert on any subject. Not in politics. Someone from Alaska can claim to be an expert on growing turnips in the desert in Arizona, having never been to the southern 48, having never seen a turnip and having no education or training in agriculture. Isn't this why we often get such poor decision-making? Marjorie Taylor-Greene is a prime example of this and the Republican party is only too happy to give her a soapbox to share her stupidity and lack of common sense and intelligence. Isn't this why politicians are often held in contempt and are viewed as corrupt even if they have never been proven to have broken the law?

Perhaps the problem is that we feel so removed from the political process. We cannot all go to a barn and vote regarding local events and cannot represent ourselves in the political arena because if we could do, the system would be completely unwieldy. So, we elect people to represent us and hope that they have an interest in doing so. I am not suggesting the past was perfect but when I was a kid our Member of Parliament returned letters and was accountable to those they served. They would tell you what they planned to do about your concerns so you felt you were being well represented. It was as close as it could be to representing yourself. The politicians could not represent differing opinions on some issues and this was understood. Many had integrity and when they said they would do something they either did it, or paid for it at the ballot box the next election. None were spewing hateful, divisive rhetoric and there was no Fox News as it is today that employs mouthpieces and gives a platform to those who support white supremacy, division and hate. Perhaps most of all politics was about issues and platforms, ideas and how different parties proposed to tackle the difficult issues of the day. There were no smear campaigns that I was aware of, and while heated debates occurred, they were kept civil because they focused on the issues and not on personalities. These were people who you may have differed with ideologically but who you could still respect because of the way in which they conducted themselves. This is in sharp contrast to many of the politicians of today in the United States in particular who engage in smear campaigns, the spreading of harmful misinformation about opponents, who promote divisions, racism and hate, or who are complicit in all of this through silence as members of their party do this. These are not people worthy of respect and that is one of the reasons the people who would best serve us in politics won't become involved. Who wants to be associated with the Boebert's, McCarthy's, Taylor-Green's, Trump's …. of the world. Who wants the embarrassment and humiliation of telling people that they have the same job as Boebert, Taylor-Green, Gosar, Jordan…? Some may think that these people are indicative of how you conduct yourself in the same position even though you have integrity, support inclusion and work toward the betterment of the country and the citizens in it.

Politics as a circus sideshow will not attract the type of people who have the skills, abilities and personalities needed to do a competent job. It is sad, and when politicians who are highly incompetent are given soapboxes, major damage can be done and is being done. It is a pity these people lack the insight to know they are destroying their country, or more likely, they just don't care because it is all about them and not the constituent, or anyone else.

The politicians doing the heavy lifting are too busy trying to do their job to spend hours spewing hate and nonsense. They are building support for legislation, writing draft legislation, representing and communicating with their constituents, attending committee meetings and doing many other things. They would be people worth listening to because they do not constantly seek attention and daily do the work necessary to improve the lives of their constituents and country.

Passive Aggressive Politics Canadian Style

I received two vaccinations and am anxious to get a booster when I get back to Canada. So, I am not an anti-vaxxer and understand perfectly well the benefits of vaccinations. Like most Canadian kids I was given several vaccinations in public school for things like polio, typhoid and tetanus. I do not profess to be an expert about Covid-19, or anything else that is of a medical or scientific nature. I agreed with almost all the measures taken by the province of British Columbia to deal with Covid-19 and feel the provincial government has done as good a job as could be done. It is important to remember Covid-19 was a moving target. As the virus was mutating and spreading scientists and medical experts were scrambling to keep up. I am not someone who does not express my opinion when I am not happy with the government but am happy to give credit where it is due. The major issue I have with the way Covid-19 was handled was the way in which it was handled by the Federal Government. I am not qualified to question the science, or the medical approach used, even if it did seem nonsensical at times. As a Canadian visiting another country, I do know that most Canadians that I encountered had no idea what the Federal government would do in regard to the travel rules for returning home. It had become a political issue Prime Minister Trudeau was hanging his hat on to try to win a majority government in a $600 million election he called only eighteen months into his term. The Liberal Government obviously thought it could ride its response to Covid-19 through another election that would give it a majority government. This was not the case in spite of Prime Minister Trudeau appearing on television every day updating Canadians on the federal government's response to Covid-19.

There were other people within the government who could have provided daily updates to Canadians but the Prime Minister chose to do so. This was not a surprise since Prime Minister Trudeau had told Canadians that if he did not get a majority government, we would be headed back to the polls in eighteen months. For obvious reasons this angered many, and the election and the $600 million bill were seen as totally unnecessary. As it turned out the $600 million dollar election resulted in another minority government for the Liberals and $600 million added to an already burgeoning deficit. Hardly good management. Perhaps Prime Minister Trudeau had thought that everyone had forgotten his three major ethical violations, his dressing up in India like an Indian, and his business trip that involved one meeting and a nice week-long holiday for his family. Then there was the invitation to a state dinner of a convicted murderer. That likely did not help Trudeau in his bid to gain a majority government.

> Atwal, who did not travel to India with the Trudeaus' entourage, was convicted of the attempted murder of an Indian cabinet minister, Malkiat Singh Sidhu, on Vancouver Island in 1986. At the time, he was a member of the International Sikh Youth Federation, banned as a terrorist group in Canada, the U.K., the U.S. and India. He was also charged, but not convicted, in a 1985 near-fatal attack on Ujjal Dosanjh, an opponent of the Sikh separatist movement who later became premier of British Columbia. More recently, he was found liable in an automobile fraud case. The

International Sikh Youth Federation was declared a terrorist organization by the Canadian government in the early 1980s. Atwal was one of four men who ambushed and shot at Sidhu's car on a rural road on Vancouver Island in 1986, badly wounding him. More recently, the Insurance Corp. of British Columbia won a $28,000 judgment against Atwal over a stolen car ring involving Atwal's son, Vik, and dozens of others. Atwal has denied any involvement in the attack on Dosanjh, but admits his role in the attempt to assassinate Sidhu. A photograph of Jaspal Atwal's invitation to attend a dinner at Canada's High Commission for Canada to India (can be seen online-author's inclusion).[15]

The point being that Prime Minister Trudeau must have felt that Canadians were happy with the government's response to Covid-19. I saw it as being unnecessarily heavy handed by a man that ran away when the anti-vaccination rules trucker's convoy arrived in Ottawa. I perceived it as an attempt by the

---

15   Terry Milewski. CBC News. *Convicted attempted murderer invited to reception with Trudeau in India*. February 21, 2018.

Prime Minister to show strength when what it did show was that for some reason the Prime Minister wanted to punish Canadians. I should qualify that by saying that he wanted to punish Canadians who were not in his economic class, in spite of his statements about understanding the poor and middle class. The reasons I say this appear below. Take the daily costs of the hotels and then multiply them by fourteen days, add the cost of your meals for fourteen days, add the GST and hotel tax and you will see that you would owe a huge amount of money. This, when there are many other hotel options that are far cheaper and could have been used for quarantine. Had the government done this, middle and working-class Canadians would have been as free to travel as the very wealthy, like Prime Minister Trudeau. It was an attempt by the government to say, "we are not taking your freedoms away but will make it impossible for anyone who is not extremely wealthy to travel. It was a form of economic segregation but then we are used to the wealthy being given special privilege by this government.

> List of Government Approved Quarantine Hotels Prices are for single occupancy (1 person). Prices are for reference only and are subject to change.

TORONTO HOTEL PRICE (PER DAY)

Four Points Sheraton $309
Alt Hotel $399
Fairfield Inn $279
Holiday Inn Toronto Airport $329
Sheraton Gateway $319

MONTRÉAL HOTEL PRICE (PER DAY)
Crowne Plaza $313

VANCOUVER HOTEL PRICE (PER DAY)

Westin Wall Centre $525
Fairmont $463
Radisson $421
Days Inn $650

Prices for hotels do not include taxes, fees or additional hotel services. Visit the government of Canada website for a full list of approved hotels.[16]

If this were not bad enough, people who failed to comply with the travel quarantine rules stood to be fined up to $750,000 and receive up to six months in jail. Obviously, the size of the potential fines

---

16 ILCS. *Canada Welcomes You, ILSC Welcomes You: Quarantine Accommodation Packages.* May 4, 2021.

communicated the message that containing the virus is serious business, and I agree wholeheartedly, however I get the message if I get a $100 speeding ticket or $30 fine. I think the size of the fines was political theatrics and the inconsistency with which the rules were applied was annoying.

What would a $750,000 dollar fine do to your life, and that of your family? I suspect the consequence to you would be far different than it would be to a wealthy family, like Prime Minister Trudeau's family. You may lose your home, car and have to claim bankruptcy. You may be thinking the fine is easily avoided so it is not a big deal. It certainly is a big deal and let me share a personal experience that could have caused me some real problems. I got my BC vaccine passport and felt I was all set to travel. I had been vaccinated twice and had the proof I needed to get on a flight when the government was easing up on the travel rules in November. A day before I was to get on the flight my BC vaccine passport was apparently no longer of any value. What did this mean? It meant that the Q code on the new Federal vaccine passport stayed exactly the same but that I had to pay more money so I could copy the same vaccine passport but now it had a little 'Canada' government logo in the top right-hand corner. When the rules are in seemingly constant flux it may have been easy to inadvertently break the rules. I could have gone to the airport and not been able to get on a flight as a result of this silly change that did not change the Q code at all. I think we all understood that it is a very serious violation to break quarantine rules but so is driving while using a cellphone, and one fine is a few hundred dollars and the other $750,000. Yes, violating a quarantine is very serious and should be dealt with harshly but if you think that the fact someone could cause a death by transmitting the virus and that justified the $750,000 fine, why then would things like impaired driving and driving while using a cellphone and other dangerous actions not be fined at the same level, given that they can, and do, cause death. It was very heavy handed and Canadians were not treated like responsible citizens who wanted to do the right thing. The government was very big on threats, theatrics and punishment but what benefits did the government provide to those who chose to get vaccinated, beyond the obvious personal health benefits.

If you have a child everyone knows that positive reinforcement and incentives are far more helpful in modifying behaviour than is punishment. One is positively oriented and the other a very negative approach. Why the Canadian Government, which is supported by Canadians and elected by Canadians who pay their wages, felt that a punishment model rather than one using positive reinforcement was appropriate is beyond me. Certainly, I can see reasonable penalties for violations and more serious penalties for those who are in serious violation, but $750,000! How about doing things like saying that those who are double vaccinated will not require PCR tests, or antigen tests when returning to Canada, or making it easier to travel for those who are doubly vaccinated. My point being that since we are all Canadians, we should be using a compassionate model based on reinforcement rather than a heavy-handed punishment orientation. Trudeau loves to play the tough guy until of course the truck convoy arrived in Ottawa.

Penalties and fines

Consequences for failure to comply with the Emergency Order

- Failure to comply with this order is an offence under the Quarantine Act and could lead to **fines, imprisonment or both.**

- Visits from law enforcement officers

Penalties, fines and imprisonment

Violating any instructions provided to you when you entered Canada is an offence under the Quarantine Act and could lead to up to:

- 6 months in prison **and/or**

- $750,000 in fines

If you break your mandatory quarantine or isolation requirements and you cause the death or serious bodily harm to another person, you could face:

- a fine of up to $1,000,000 **or**

- imprisonment of up to 3 years **or**

- both

The Contraventions Act provides police (including RCMP, provincial and local police) the authority to enforce the *Quarantine Act*. Tickets with fines of up to $5,000 may be issued for non-compliance.

If you receive a fine, **you must still** comply fully with the mandatory testing and quarantine requirements outlined in the *Quarantine, Isolation and Other Obligations*

Order. Additionally, if you receive a fine, you're considered at high-risk of non-compliance, and flagged as a high priority for follow up by local law enforcement.[17]

I don't deny that there should be stiff fines but should forgetting to wear a mask on one occasion warrant a fine in the thousands of dollars? If someone is fined $1,000,000 for causing serious bodily harm or death by failing to follow Covid-19 quarantine rules, does the money go to the government, or the family who has lost a loved one? If it goes to the government, it may be hard for the relatives of the victim to sue the person who caused one of their family to die because they will already owe the government a million dollars. The other issue with this is that Border Services have no oversight and these are additional powers. I don't know about you but I have always had more difficulty getting back into Canada than entering any other country, and I am Canadian. On the trip I just took I experienced a new approach by Border Services. I had given my boarding pass to the airline attendant just prior to entering the tunnel to board the plane and started to proceed into the tunnel where I was met by three

---

17   Government of Canada. *Quarantine or Isolation.* March 8, 2022.

Border Security officers. They asked me if I had $10,000 on me. I told them I was not into money laundering. I wanted to say that if you are interested in money laundering you may want to look into the report about organized crime laundering $5 billion a year in BC but thought better of it. This after a scowling Border security official had told me that I was in violation of the rules for trying to take too much sunscreen and toothpaste in my carry-on luggage. I was unaware of the rule so was happy to depart with it and the scowling was unnecessary. The best people in positions of authority are polite and courteous and know they have authority they can use if required. In the meantime, they are courteous and efficient. Again, we are all Canadians. Rather than using a punitive model that often seems to attract those who enjoy intimidating others and exercising power over them, they could use a positive reinforcement/educational model where possible. For example, rather than treating me like an attempted criminal they could have simply told me the rules about the limits for liquids in carry-on luggage, taken mine from me and I may have thanked them for educating me about the rules.

> Why is positive reinforcement more effect-
> ive than punishment?

People often find positive reinforcement easier to swallow than other methods of training, since it doesn't involve taking anything away or introducing a negative consequence. It's also **much easier to encourage behaviours than to discourage them**, making reinforcement a more powerful tool than punishment in most cases.[18]

This is true and as I mentioned it works with children and you can see a massive difference between a child that has been brought up with positive reinforcement rather than continual punishment. Positive reinforcement results in less conflict, better future outcomes and a sense that one is being treated as a fellow Canadian by another Canadian, even if they do have a job to do that at times will involve the use of authority. After all, 99% of us do not want weapons and drugs brought into the country or taken to other countries by Canadians. It is all in the approach and presumably in the recruitment process, training and lack of government oversight that has led to the government's orientation of punishment, rather than positive reinforcement. The excessively

---

18   Courtenay E. Ackerman, M.A. Positive Psychology. *Positive Reinforcement in Psychology* (definition + 5 examples). February 4, 2022.

expensive quarantine hotels, excessive fines and general approach of the Canadian Government was passive-aggressive in terms of dealing with violators of the Covid-19 rules, and make no mistake it was aggressive and the rules were such that they could force someone into bankruptcy through a series of errors, or through not adhering to rules that could change with little notice.

Surely, the heavy-handed approach by the Trudeau government did not increase his popularity prior to the last election. I talked with a number of people who saw the hotel quarantine rules economically segregating Canadians and favouring the wealthy over everyone else. The haves could travel and the have-nots could not. Of course, Prime Minister Trudeau is a have and has been throughout his entire life. I suspect this is why cheaper accommodations were not sought for quarantining Canadians.

Someone Else's Fault

One of the least effective ways to solve problems is to look for external sources to blame. Like divorcees where each partner blames the other and takes no responsibility for the failure of a marriage. It is hardly a formula to avoid future relationship issues and no learning takes place due to a total lack of insight, coupled with denial. That combined with lying to oneself and others about the true nature of the problems will ensure that nothing changes for the better. Is this not what we see in politics? There is an appalling lack of insight and reflection into what is happening in politics by those involved. Either that, or they simply don't care. Moral and ethical bankruptcy may also explain the behavior of some politicians. Age does not ensure that politicians have the ability to operate at a level where the implications of their actions on others are considered. A great deal of what has been occurring with those on the extreme right within the Republican party may be accurately referred to as infantile, unless of course there are mental illnesses involved that better serve to explain their behavior. Kohlberg's levels of moral reasoning are quite helpful in determining the maturity and moral development levels of people like Marjorie Taylor-Green, Jordan, Cruz, Boebert, Gaetz and other Republican party members. When you add in attention-seeking, making juvenile threats and blaming others for problems, at best, these people are operating at Level 1, Stage 2 of Kohlberg's Levels of Moral Reasoning. It is the level where children only reciprocate if it helps meet their needs. Does this sound like Donald Trump's transactional relationships where he will only do something for others if there is something in it for him? It does fit well with the lies and tantrums. In Trump's case this sort of behavior may result from a narcissistic personality disorder but its appearance is still very childish.

Kohlberg's Theory of Moral Development

Level 1. Pre-conventional Morality

Stage 1 – Obedience and Punishment The earliest stage of moral development is especially common in young children, but adults are also capable of expressing this type of reasoning. At this stage, children see rules as fixed and absolute. Obeying the rules is important because it is a means to avoid punishment.

Stage 2 – Individualism and Exchange At this stage of moral development, children account for individual points of view and judge actions based on how they serve individual needs. In the Heinz dilemma, children argued that the best course of action was the choice that best-served Heinz's needs. Reciprocity is possible, but only if it serves one's own interests.

Level 2. Conventional Morality

Stage 3 – Interpersonal Relationships Often referred to as the "good boy-good girl" orientation, this stage of moral development is focused on living up to social expectations and roles. There is an emphasis on conformity, being "nice," and consideration of how choices influence relationships.

Stage 4 – Maintaining Social Order At this stage of moral development, people begin to consider society as a whole when making judgments. The focus is on maintaining law and order by following the rules, doing one's duty and respecting authority.

Level 3. Post-conventional Morality

Stage 5 – Social Contract and Individual Rights At this stage, people begin to account for the differing values, opinions and beliefs of other people. Rules of law are important for maintaining a society, but members of the society should agree upon these standards.

Stage 6 – Universal Principles Kolhberg's final level of moral reasoning is based upon universal ethical principles and abstract reasoning. At this stage, people follow these internalized principles of justice, even if they conflict with laws and rules.[19]

Ideally politicians should be operating at no less than Level 3, Stages 5 and 6. Many fall woefully short. Then there are others who are difficult to place on the scale because not only do they only act out of self-interest, but they try to undermine the Constitution, minimize acts of violence like the January 6

---

19   Wikipedia. *Kohlberg's Theory of Moral Development.*

insurrection and lie about Donald Trump winning the last election, when Joe Biden did. Perhaps people like this do not even fit on the scale because they are morally and ethically bankrupt. It is beyond self-centredness and extends into deliberately harming others and their country. When a country has a lot of politicians operating at Level 1, Stage 2 we should not be surprised by their infantile behaviour. Boebert and Taylor-Green are prime examples. Along with the infantile behaviour often comes nothing being done that is constructive in terms of creating and influencing policy, drafting legislation, looking for non-partisan solutions etc. No, it is attention-seeking and in some cases such extreme selfishness that they harm their own party but apparently could care less.

> On the basis of his research, Kohlberg identified six stages of moral reasoning grouped into three major levels. Each level represented a fundamental shift in the social-moral perspective of the individual. At the first level, the preconventional level, a person's moral judgments are characterized by a concrete, individual perspective. Within this level, a Stage 1 heteronomous orientation focuses on avoiding breaking rules that are backed by punishment,

obedience for its own sake and avoiding the physical consequences of an action to persons and property. As in Piaget's framework, the reasoning of Stage 1 is characterized by ego-centrism and the inability to consider the perspectives of others. At Stage 2 there is the early emergence of moral reciprocity. The Stage 2 orientation focuses on the instrumental, pragmatic value of an action. Reciprocity is of the form, "you scratch my back and I'll scratch yours." The Golden Rule becomes, "If someone hits you, you hit them back." At Stage 2 one follows the rules only when it is to someone's immediate interests. What is right is what's fair in the sense of an equal exchange, a deal, an agreement. At Stage 2 there is an understanding that everybody has his(her) own interest to pursue and these conflicts, so that right is relative (in the concrete individualist sense). Individuals at the conventional level of reasoning, however, have a basic understanding of conventional morality, and reason with an understanding that norms and conventions are necessary to uphold society. They tend to be self-identified with these rules, and uphold them consistently, viewing morality as acting in accordance with what society defines as right.[20]

When you have many people in the Republican Party operating at Level 1 it is easy to see the problem. It also explains the ousting of those in the party who are operating at a higher level of moral reasoning. Those who think in terms of the Constitution, other people, and who have a higher level of moral reasoning will not blindly adhere to the whims of Donald Trump, and that is perceived as a problem by Trump and others in the party. Not only have there been attempts to oust these people from the party, but great care has been taken by Trump to support Republicans who will oppose the Republican politicians in primaries who have failed to blindly adhere to whatever he directs. Donald Trump has become a cult leader and those who will not support his lies, conspiracy theories and misinformation need to be expelled from the party. So, the party is extremely unhealthy and the divide within the Republican party reminds me of the division in the country that threatens to rip it apart. The extremists in the party

---

20   Wikipedia. *Kohlberg's Theory of Moral Development.*

are not being reigned in presumably because they are being supported by Donald Trump. This may be fine within the Republican party but people like Boebert, Taylor-Greene, Jordan and others are hurting the party. For the Republicans to win the next election they will need the support of some moderates and soft Democrats. The rhetoric from the extreme right in the Republican party makes it far less likely that they will gain this vital support. This is because there are millions of United States voters who are not white supremacists, who like democracy, who are not buying the lies, misinformation and conspiracy theories and who would like to return to sane democratic politics. They were also angered by the January 6 insurrection and see Trump as being responsible for it.

To give you a few examples of the type of moral reasoning in today's politics, let's have a look at the sales of weapons to Saudi Arabia. This country is known for killing a journalist, human rights violations and for creating huge numbers of refugees in Yemen, yet the Canadian government has on more than one occasion tried to justify sales of weapons to it. Just before you see what the Canadian government has been doing, ask yourself this simple question. If I were to give you a gun knowing full well that you had gunned down innocent people, and you then shot and killed someone, am I complicit in the murder since I provided the weapon that you used to kill someone? Is it even worse than complicit, since I knew you had a history of killing innocent people? Can you see any way to morally or ethically justify my sale of the gun to you since I knew you had previously killed innocent people?

The Canadian government is clearly complicit in the loss of innocent lives in Yemen based on the same reasoning. We cannot give people the means to harm others and then pretend we have no responsibility when people are inevitably harmed. The level of moral reasoning for acts like this is extremely low because selling weapons is all about Canadian companies and people making money without regard for those who will be killed as a result. I do not hold the people who make weapons responsible but do hold the government responsible for approving the sales of weapons to countries with histories of horrific internal and external human rights abuses.

In terms of the legitimacy to govern we have a Prime Minister who does not hesitate to call out other countries for their human rights abuses in spite of all the graves of residential school children being dug up, and selling weapons to regimes that we know commit atrocities. Before Canada wants to get on its high horse about ethical, moral and human rights abuses it may want to clean up its own backyard first. Prime Minister Trudeau should not be in government because a leader should have a moral and ethical compass, but Trudeau's behaviour indicates he is devoid of one. How can you sell weapons to a country that is killing innocent people and even try to justify this in any way. Economics are far too frequently used to excuse the irresponsible actions of governments. I would rather have no economic benefits than see more poor Yemen people become refugees.

Human Rights Watch in its 2014 report alleged the government of Saudi Arabia remains a serial abuser of human rights.

"Saudi Arabia stepped up arrests, trials, and convictions of peaceful dissidents, and forcibly dispersed peaceful demonstrations by citizens in 2013," the report said.

"Authorities continued to violate the rights of nine million Saudi women and girls and nine million foreign workers ... As in past years, authorities subjected thousands of people to unfair trials and arbitrary detention."

Saudi Arabia permits beheading and stoning

as forms of criminal punishment for murder and rape, alongside social crimes such as adultery. Homosexual acts are also punishable by death, flogging and imprisonment, as is drug use. Saudi Arabia is also regularly condemned for its treatment of women, who will earn the right to vote in 2015, but who will still be disallowed from driving cars — or armoured vehicles, for that matter.

In a statement today, London, Ont., Conservative MP Susan Truppe praised the deal. Truppe, who is also the parliamentary secretary for the Status of Women, said the deal proved the Conservative government was acting on job creation and not just spouting empty rhetoric.

"I am thrilled that our government has announced that London will be the primary beneficiary of the largest advanced manufacturing export win in our nation's history," she said.

The government and GDLS say the Saudi deal will create and sustain more than 3,000 jobs a year for 14 years and will benefit 500 Canadian companies. Its value could climb to nearly $14 billion if all options are exercised.[21]

Yes, but they forgot to mention how many innocent people will lose their lives as a result. Nor did they mention the contradiction between MP Truppe being involved with the Status of Women and condoning the sale of weapons to a country that severely oppresses women and makes women in Yemen refugees. Are we just supposed to ignore that uncomfortable fact! Are we to celebrate this deal and then watch the horrific things we see in Yemen and be happy about Canada's complicity in it? It shows that the Liberal and Conservative governments that approved these weapon sales are morally and ethically bankrupt. Or is the thinking that because Yemen is a poor country people are expendable in the same way that the poor and homeless in Canada have become under multiple governments? Perhaps worse than the weapons sales themselves are the attempts by politicians to justify them when there is no justification.

> Canada sold a record amount of military hardware to Saudi Arabia in 2019, despite sharply criticizing its poor human rights

---

21   James Cudmore. CBC News. *General Dynamics Canada wins $10 B deal with Suadi Arabia.* February 14, 2014.

record and placing a moratorium on any new exports to the kingdom.

Newly released figures show Canada sold nearly C$3bn (US$2.2bn) worth of military equipment to Saudi Arabia in 2019 – more than double the total of the previous year, reported the Globe and Mail. The bulk of the exports were light armoured vehicles, part of a deal with the Saudis worth C$14.8bn.

The record figures come despite a moratorium on export permits following the killing of the Saudi journalist Jamal Khashoggi and mounting civilian deaths from the war in Yemen. The government's decision not to issue new permits does not affect existing permits. A permit can cover multiple items and as a result, companies have existing permits for years.

Justin Trudeau says Canada is looking to pull out of Saudi arms deal

"I struggle to know what 'moratorium' means to this government, because to me, when there's a moratorium on something, you can't increase the sales of that thing.

And exactly what seems to have happened," said Mark Kersten, deputy director of the Wayamo Foundation.

"I can't understand for the life of me, why the government wouldn't say anything about it, unless it just simply didn't want the public to know, because it looks awful."

Canada also exported more than 30 large-calibre artillery systems and 152 heavy machine guns to Saudi Arabia.

The multi-billion-dollar arms deal with the kingdom was initiated under a previous Conservative government in 2014, but continued under the Liberals.

At the time it was signed, it was the largest export deal in Canada's history, making the country the second-largest arms exporter to the Middle East.

Rights groups, academics and policy advisers have long called on Trudeau to cancel the deal, and follow the example of Germany and Sweden which both cancelled arms contracts with Saudi Arabia following public outrage over Khashoggi's murder.

The Liberal government argued that Canada would incur billions of dollars in penalties if it tore up the contract.

After a government review, the foreign affairs minister, François-Philippe Champagne, said in April that there was no clear evidence that Canadian military hardware was being used for human rights violations in Saudi Arabia.

"Maybe this government thinks that Canadians won't judge it by successes or failures abroad, that they'll ultimately win re-election based on what happens domestically," said Kersten. "And so you end up in a situation where the government makes working with this horrible criminal regime an issue of taxpayers and jobs – and not about a courageous feminist foreign policy or the image of Canada itself."[22]

Yes, that is precisely what has happened. Canada never should have entered into this deal in

22   Leyland Cecco. The Guardian. *Canada doubles weapons sale to Saudi Arabia despite moratorium.* June 9, 2020.

the first place and it is a little late for Trudeau to be trying to claim a moral position since a journalist was killed by the Saudis. Trudeau had an opportunity to act morally when the Liberals took power and could have cancelled the deal but chose not to. For political expediency, Canada has sold weapons to a regime known for a variety of human rights abuses and in the process has smeared Canada's international reputation. We used to be a peace-keeping nation and we still claim to be morally and ethically superior to other countries with human rights abuses, but this type of thing puts us in the same category. Not only that but the Prime Minister claims to be a strong supporter of women's rights, yet, Saudi Arabia is known for its oppression of women. Rather than making a statement about this to try to improve the lives of women in Saudi Arabia the government says nothing and sells them weapons.

Economic justifications are not justifications at all. How would you feel if your family was killed with weapons from Russia so that some people would have jobs there? Would you feel this justified the deaths of your family members? The point being that we live in a global community and there are no expendable people. Being poor does not mean that it is okay to kill you because it benefits a wealthy country economically. I am embarrassed to be a Canadian and wish I could do something to help the poor people of Yemen. Being a Canadian, I am complicit in the deaths of innocent people in Yemen based on the actions of my government.

> The war in Yemen broke out in late 2014 when Houthi rebels seized large swaths of the country, including the capital, Sanaa. The conflict escalated in March 2015 when Saudi Arabia and the United Arab Emirates assembled a military coalition in an attempt to restore the government of Riyadh-backed President Abd-Rabbu Mansour Hadi.

> The ongoing war has pushed millions to the brink of famine in what the United Nations has described as the world's worst humanitarian crisis, and at least 233,000 people have died, according to a recent UN estimate.

> "There is persuasive evidence that weapons exported from Canada to KSA [Kingdom of Saudi Arabia], including LAVs [light-armoured vehicles] and sniper rifles, have been diverted for use in the war in Yemen," Wednesday's report found.

"Given the overriding risk posed by Canadian weapons exports to KSA, Canada must immediately revoke existing arms export permits to KSA and suspend the issuance of new ones."[23]

Is it a shock that items purportedly provided to a country for one use are being used for another? We have seen this happen and the Canadian government surely knew this was likely and predictable. To pretend it is surprising would be like giving a country uranium for a power plant and then pretending to be shocked that they have created a nuclear weapon instead. Given the history of the Saudis should we pretend to be surprised by deception? I hardly think so!

> But for years, Canadian civil society groups have urged the federal government to cancel existing weapons contracts with Saudi Arabia and suspend all future permits, arguing that the arms could be used in rights violations both inside the Gulf nation and in Yemen.

---

23   Al Jazeera Staff. *Canada Violating Int'l Law by Selling Weapons to Saudis: Report.* August 11, 2021.

In particular, rights groups have urged Canada to cancel a $12bn ($15bn Canadian) weapons contract to ship Canadian-made LAVs to the Saudi government.

That deal was reached under former Prime Minister Stephen Harper, but Trudeau's government gave it the final green light. Early into his tenure as prime minister, Trudeau had defended the exports, saying they were consistent with the country's human rights obligations and foreign policy.

The conflict in Yemen has pushed millions to the brink of famine in what the United Nations has described as the world's worst humanitarian crisis [File: Ali Owidha/ Reuters]

But in the aftermath of the murder of prominent Saudi journalist Jamal Khashoggi in 2018, he said his government was looking for a way out of the deal – and Ottawa ordered a review of weapons exports to Riyadh.

Khashoggi, a Washington Post columnist, was assassinated by a Saudi hit squad in

October 2018 at the country's consulate in Istanbul. International experts and more recently, United States intelligence agencies, concluded that Saudi Crown Prince Mohammed bin Salman, the country's de facto leader, approved the operation. The Saudi government has denied that allegation.

Despite global pressure after the killing, in April 2020 the Canadian government lifted its freeze on weapons export permits to Saudi Arabia after a review, saying it had a robust system in place to ensure such permits meet Canada's requirements under domestic law and the ATT.[24]

If the sale of these weapons was "consistent" with Canada's human right policy, our human right policy is not worth the paper it is written on. Canada's justification of the continued sales of weapons is a disgrace and there are no justifications for this. These ongoing sales simply confirm what we knew all along. Money dictates what happens in the world and Canada's government, led by a man with two

---

24   Al Jazeera Staff. *Canada Violating Int'l Law by Selling Weapons to Saudis: Report.* August 11, 2021.

major ethical violations, lacks ethics and morality, and puts money before human life. Ask yourself what type of people would do this? Aside from 3,000 workers in London, who this government is representing, surely most Canadians do not want to be complicit in the deaths of innocent people. We see an ongoing movement toward unethical and immoral politics. I must be old school because I think they have a lot to do with the legitimacy to govern and our government seems devoid of the positive attributes and ethical conduct that would give it the legitimacy to govern. I cannot tell you how many times the Prime Minister has behaved in ways that should embarrass all Canadians. I feel that as Canadians we are better than this, and as the world is thrown into a massive international mess of senseless attacks on Ukraine, Trump lies and right-wing populism, I had hoped that Canada could provide a positive light and do the right things when others need support, hope and moral and ethical leadership. The sad reality is that we cannot play that role when we engage in this type of irresponsibility. When it comes to selling weapons to countries with records of human rights abuses the United States is also heavily involved. In spite of the Democrats acting as if they are on the side of morality and ethics, President Biden has been approving the sales of weapons to countries many feel should not have them.

The Biden administration notified Congress in June of a proposed sale of more than $2.5 billion in arms to the Philippines, including fighter jets and two kinds of precision missiles. The notice came less than two weeks after the International Criminal Court prosecutor sought approval to open a formal investigation into crimes against humanity related to the Philippines' brutal "war on drugs."

Human rights groups promptly expressed concern that the administration would reward an increasingly abusive government with such a large weapons sale, particularly given public pledges by both President Biden and Secretary of State Antony Blinken that the new administration would put human rights at the center of U.S. foreign policy.

This is not the first time in the Biden administration's short tenure that it has found itself the object of criticism following an arms sale announcement. In February, the United States approved plans to sell Egypt missiles worth $197 million. In May, news broke of an approved arms sale worth $735 million of precision-guided weapons to Israel amid its latest military offensive in Gaza, where it used large, precision-guided munitions to destroy multi-story buildings containing scores of businesses and homes on the pretext of some unproven Hamas presence at those sites. According to the United Nations, Israeli airstrikes in May killed 260 Palestinians in Gaza, at least 129 of whom were civilians, including 66 children.

To put it bluntly, the Biden administration is selling weapons to at least three human rights abusers — the Philippines, Egypt and Israel— despite a pledge to make human rights central to its foreign policy.[25]

The Philippine military has long been responsible for serious abuses in its counterinsurgency operations, including the extrajudicial killing of political activists, peasant organizers and Indigenous

---

25   Elisa Epstein. Washington Post. *It's time for the US to stop selling weapons to human rights abusers.* July 21, 2021.

leaders. It has also engaged in "red-tagging," accusing leftist activists of links to the communist insurgency, frequently resulting in the activists' murders.

The government of President Rodrigo Duterte has been unwilling to acknowledge abuses let alone address them, and the Biden administration did not tie the sale to any conditions — at least not publicly. The day after the notification, the head of the Philippines police announced the creation of a new armed militia to be a "force multiplier" to assist counterinsurgency efforts and the "drug war."

Arms sales and $1.3 billion in annual security assistance to Egypt are continuing despite years of deteriorating human rights conditions under President Abdel Fatah al-Sissi, from probable war crimes in a protracted military campaign in North Sinai, to thousands of dissidents arbitrarily detained, indefinitely held, and subjected to torture and other ill treatment.

The Egyptian government has not even feigned pursuing accountability for the widespread and systematic killings of at least 1,150 demonstrators in 2013, at least 817 of them in one day at one protest site. In fact, days before this latest arms sale was announced, Egyptian officials raided the homes of human rights defender Mohamed Soltan's family in Egypt, arbitrarily detained several of his cousins.

The Gaza conflict took place against the backdrop of escalating repression of Palestinians in occupied East Jerusalem, including use of excessive force against worshipers at al-Aqsa Mosque, and discriminatory efforts by Israeli authorities to remove Palestinian families from their homes — policies and actions that are part of the Israeli government's crimes against humanity of apartheid and persecution.[26]

Obviously, sometimes there are strategic considerations when weapons are sold to certain countries. The Philippines, for example, is in a critical location with respect to activities and claims around ownership of the South China Sea. At times there

---

26   Elisa Epstein. Washington Post. *It's time for the US to stop selling weapons to human rights abusers*. July 21, 2021.

are trade-offs but the question is, what is being done to curb human rights abuses in the countries being sold weapons of war? How can it be known that these weapons will not be used to kill innocent people and wouldn't the world just be a better place if there was a global moratorium on the sale of weapons to any country. I can see one country giving another weapons, like in the case of Ukraine, where the country did not instigate the war with Russia but needs the means to defend itself. Are we at a point where we are so collectively devoid of morals and ethics that all weapons sales are a good thing regardless of the consequences? Are people who are complicit in the killing of innocent people fit to govern? Is this not complicity in mass murder in some instances, and does that not essentially revoke the legitimacy to govern, and if not, shouldn't it? Shouldn't people who approve these sales be taken to the International Court of the Hague and held accountable for the deaths they are complicit in?

There is another issue around these types of weapons sales that is problematic. The reasons for selling the Ukraine weapons are obvious, and most North Americans support these sales because Ukraine is on the front-line fighting for democracy for all democratic countries. We are in it together although levels of support vary. When weapons are sold to a country, we may think that there must be a good reason. We are not privy to national intelligence, or what goes on behind closed doors in terms of diplomacy. This secrecy is necessary in most instances but it would be nice to know the justifications for all arms sales beyond economic ones. I say this because economics does not justify killing innocent people. When we do not have this information, we may fill in the blanks and this is where misinformation, speculation and conspiracy theories can come into it. This is especially true in the United States where Trump has promoted the concept of the deep state and a horrible world behind the scenes that has not been proven to exist.

Clandestine activities and the mass sale of weapons when we do not know why leaves us guessing and making assumptions in lieu of any reasonable explanation. This in its own way damages democracy because the majority of us would not support the killing of other people with weapons we have sold to another country. So, when you combine the secrecy with the fact that most people in democracies do not support the mass sales of weapons in most instances, we see democratic governments like the U.S and Canadian ones acting in ways not supported by the people who elected them. This leads to the thinking that there is another world behind the scenes that we do not understand, and then it is not a great leap to start believing in the deep state, QAnon and other conspiracy theories.

Should it surprise anyone that the sale of weapons to kill innocent people, major ethical and moral violations along with a Prime Minister who likes playing dress-up has brought the Liberal party's legitimacy to govern into question. When people have no respect for the government it can be extremely problematic. The Prime Minister lied about going to Tofino and in the process disrespected First Nations who were digging up the graves of children who had been in residential school. He hid when the anti-vaccination regulations convoy went to Ottawa, Trudeau's legitimacy to govern has been brought seriously into question. In a democracy it is critical that the electorate respect the government and its right to govern, but aside from the vote count, and the Liberals actually lost the popular vote in two elections, the government has embarrassed Canadians repeatedly. As I say this, I should point out, if you had not already concluded this, that I am left-wing in my thinking and beliefs, so would be more likely to support the Liberals than the Conservatives but I cannot support either. Both were involved in arms deals and both have demonstrated over time to be morally and ethically bankrupt. It seems the tolerance for abuses has been raised after Trump came to power but I believe that in order to save democracy there should be a very low tolerance for this. There need to be real consequences for ethical violations of the type that Prime Minister Trudeau engaged in. I believe the present Canadian government has lost the legitimacy to govern. We had better hope that we are not confronted with an event that requires that the Federal government instigate a massive collective response to it, because many people have no respect for the Federal government for obvious reasons, as evidenced by the truckers refusing to leave Ottawa.

Having a government like the present Canadian government is akin to having a boss that continually acts unethically and in ways that embarrass their company and colleagues but still feels he should be afforded respect because he is the boss. Respect is earned and so too is the loss of it. The Liberal government has done an excellent job of the latter.

What Now?

I am glad that the government is providing support to Ukraine. It is the right thing to do. I am glad that we are accepting immigrants from Ukraine and are shipping food and other necessities to Ukraine. I am happy about all the sanctions placed on Russia. That is what Canadians expect. The vast majority of Canadians and Americans would like to be part of the solution. This is a good step in that direction. Now if the arms sales to countries with horrific records of human rights abuses would stop, it would be far easier to be proud of the country. Canada was known for its peacekeeping when other countries entered into conflicts. That too was an honourable role that all Canadians could take pride in. It makes no sense however, to be promoting peace out of one side of the government's mouth and promoting arm sales that create chaos and war out of the other. Legitimacy to govern is about trying to do the right thing and being part of the solution to domestic and global issues, rather than being part of the problem. It is about putting principles before money and being morally and ethically consistent.

When a country has money as its God, morals and ethics often take a back seat and the economic benefits of transactions are viewed as being good in spite of the negative consequences some cause. I feel good as a Canadian because we are helping Ukraine. I have no doubt that it is the right thing to do and feel that the government is doing an excellent job of representing all Canadians through Canada's humanitarian and military aid and economic sanctions geared toward helping Ukraine. If Canada can continue with this approach to global issues and stop things like weapons sales, and do positive things like giving all First Nations clean drinking water and helping the homeless and impoverished, I think we will be on the way to collectively feeling that the government is doing a good job of representing what it means to be Canadian.

While I criticized the Canadian government for its heavy-handed approach, Covid-19 was a new phenomenon and there was not a lot of research initially to guide responses to this deadly virus. Aside from the heavy-handed approach used by the Federal government and some inconsistencies, I think Covid-19 was handled quite well and certainly far better than it was under the Trump administration. I am pleased to see some travel restrictions lifted and was happy to see that the government did not resort to violence to deal with the anti-vaccine rules convoy in Ottawa. So, like anything else there are always positive and negative aspects to any government. We all make errors in our jobs and when they are made at the highest levels of government there can be severe consequences for Canada and other countries, like Yemen. To gain legitimacy to govern within the context I am using it in, there simply needs to be an approach taken by the government that includes the perspective "do no harm" and help where we can. We must get off the merry-go-round of money dictating what we do as a country. Canada can be a major part of the solution to some of the world's most pressing problems but to do that we must consistently have the respect of other nations. Cleaning up our own backyard with respect to the abuses of various ethnic groups and First Nations will be a good start. This process requires acknowledgement of the abuses, apologies, and if necessary, compensation. It is like doing a personal moral inventory and then apologizing to those we have harmed as we mentally pledge to do better. I think Canada is responding well to some of its history but in some cases has done things like fighting Human Rights Tribunal decisions that call for compensation being given to First Nations for the chronically inequitable funding of education and other services for First Nation's children.

Some things are worth paying for and righting historical wrongs and adhering to the principles of the Constitution are two of them. If all Canadians are equal, then surely all children should have been funded equitably for things like education and child welfare. This was not the case and while the government did not want to compensate First Nations for this inequity, failure to do so makes me wonder if the Constitution is only relevant when it is consistent with what the government chooses to do, or in this case, not do. I thought this issue was a no-brainer because of our Constitution, the documented inequities and that there are no moral or ethical arguments for failure to compensate. I can see the government trying to ensure that compensation is commensurate with years of involvement in the school system but should agree to compensation and then sort out the details. To date this has not happened. Again, an issue like this gives the Prime Minister less legitimacy when he talks about human rights abuses in other countries. Getting these past abuses dealt with in a good way increases Canada's legitimacy abroad and gives the country a more powerful position when becoming involved in issues of an international nature. It also clearly lets our indigenous people know we are sorry for the damage that has been caused to them and we wish for them to have the resources to address the intergenerational impacts of the abuses directed toward them in the past. We also need to dramatically improve relations with indigenous people in Canada and the government needs a long-term plan to address poverty, issues related to food security in the north, housing, economic sustainability etc. This will be a long-term project obviously. No plan is a formula for genocide because poverty, little economic opportunity and a host of other issues result in many health and social problems that will ultimately kill off isolated communities if not addressed.

I think most Canadians were surprised by the extent and severity of abuse that took place in residential schools across the country. As I did research for another book I became more aware of abuses of the Chinese, Japanese, East Indians, Blacks and foreign workers, many of whom are from Asia and Mexico. What I was reading did not fit with the image I had had of Canada. I am not sure how we have been able to generally view our fellow Canadians as good people who are moral and ethical and who can serve as an example to other nations. Of course, no country likes to discuss negative aspects of its histories and these tend to never make it into school texts. Nevertheless, while Canada has done peacekeeping and has tried to do the right thing on many occasions when there is international strife, we, like most other countries, have aspects of our history we would just as soon others did not know about. I think it was good to learn about many negative aspects of Canada's history because it tempered my sense of moral superiority, promoted through the idea that Canada is inherently good and is above human rights abuses, horrible racism, abuse of minority groups and a host of other things. It made me rethink what it meant to be a Canadian and made me think that we need to do better. I love Canada, and compared to living in many countries I have been incredibly fortunate. I know this, but also know where we have come from as a country. There are underlying elements in Canada, as we have seen in the United States, that are harmful, and if given the chance, will take Canada to places most of us have no desire to go.

I thought about the issue of the legitimacy to govern, in part, because I wondered if Canada has improved on its historical abuses, or if it is just an illusion. How will history judge government actions today?

It seems we like to make assumptions about who we are as a people and how we somehow can serve as a self-appointed moral compass for others. This is similar to United States citizens stating that they come from the greatest country on earth. What is the measure? Surely, making these types of assumptions is subjective at best and is based on ignorance, a lack of information, or an ignoring of obvious facts, like for example, gun violence being way out of control in the United States. We create myths and legends that make us feel comfortable because they conveniently omit many facts about history and who we really are as a people.

It is problematic to measure, what today we consider historical abuses against todays standards, although things like sexual abuse were not acceptable in the past, or today. Spankings on the other hand were totally acceptable and even encouraged by some in the past, whereas today they are frowned upon. While it is true standards of conduct change, so it seems too do standards of what is acceptable conduct in politics. Some may argue that Sir John A. McDonald engaged in various abuses and was involved in the start of residential schools, and so may disagree that political standards of conduct have become more lenient. When you consider what President Donald Trump and Prime Minister Trudeau have gotten away with and have still enjoyed high levels of support it is obvious there is a huge tolerance and acceptance of political abuses. Perhaps there have been so many abuses that "politics" and "political abuse" are one and the same. Quite sad that we overlook such horrific abuses, although when there is a chronic lack of competent and ethical politicians, we are forced to choose between candidates in terms of who will do the least damage. I would say the same of the United States but the United States is not a democracy and may very well be on its way to a dictatorial government in one of its many forms.

Governments are like marriages. In good marriages there is trust and in bad ones there is not. Some governments can be trusted and the citizenry, in common vernacular, feels the government has their back no matter how grave the situation is. Other governments cannot be trusted and things like lying about being in Ottawa when on the way to Tofino and skipping out on a very important First Nations event did not lend trust to Trudeau, or his government. Leaving the Ottawa area when the anti-vaccine regulations convoy came to Ottawa did not leave Canadians feeling that the Prime Minister had their back and led me to wonder where he may go, given a more serious situation like a war.

Like in a bad marriage, Canadians were abandoned during the trucker convoy problems in Ottawa and it was hugely disappointing. This was particularly true after Prime Minister Trudeau went out of his way to abuse his power with the monstrous fines, I referred to earlier for Covid-19 violations. He played the tough guy when no one was in Ottawa causing problems and made it very difficult for Canadians, other than those in his class to travel, or return to the country, but as soon as there was a potential threat he fled. This is typical bullying behaviour where the bully likes to play tough guy until he is threatened and then runs away.

This is in stark contrast to the President of Ukraine, Volodymyr Zelenskyy who has shown tremendous courage in the face of ongoing vicious, unwarranted attacks from Russia. Trudeau had some transport trucks in Ottawa, while Zelenskyy could be easily killed at any time in the horrible indiscriminate bombings by Russia. Zelenskyy is a man that has been there for his people. I do not know what kind of President he has been, or his record, but what I do know is that when his country needed him, he was there, and has continued to be there through all the horrible senseless killings and nightmare of ongoing Russian attacks on civilians, a maternity hospital, school and so on. If Trudeau felt the need to hide during the truck convoy, what would he have done in Zelenskyy's position? The legitimacy to govern is not about fair-weather governance when the leader is present when all is well, but pulls a disappearing act when it is not. We don't elect leaders to operate like this and when they do, they, a) show how inept they are, and b) show that they are not leaders at all.

I am not versed at all in Ukraine politics and do not know how they work, or the complexities of them. What I do believe is that right now President Zelenskyy has the respect and admiration of the Ukraine people because of his courage and leadership. He has the legitimacy to govern beyond his legal mandate to do so. Prime Minister Trudeau does not in spite of being elected. Perhaps the best way to explain this would be to pretend that there is a massive crisis in Canada and everyone needs to be mobilized to respond to the threat. Would you be more likely to follow Trudeau, with his lies, three major ethical violations and cowardice, or someone like President Zelenskyy? That is the difference in the legitimacy to govern. Why does Zelenskyy have the legitimacy to govern? It is all about personal attributes and behaviour that gives him legitimacy and the power to lead through example. People allow themselves to be led because they trust that he is doing the best that he can for Ukraine. If

Russia attacked Canada, I hope that Prime Minister Trudeau will stick around and try to lead, but I don't know if he would, or if people would allow him to lead given his history and poor judgement. So, beyond the legal requirements to have the legitimacy to govern it is about strength of character, personal attributes and demonstrating leadership when in critical and dangerous situations. These are comparisons made based on what I know about the President of Ukraine and are specific to his war efforts. I have no idea how the Ukraine population sees him in other contexts, whether he is honest or corrupt etc. Winston Church-ill was not a pleasant person but he had the legitimacy to govern Britain during the Second World War and if had not, I hate to think where we would be today.

Avoiding the Obvious

Human beings hate to admit to failure. It is much easier and more comfortable to seek external answers to problems and issues that require internal solutions. Looking inside ourselves for solutions to internal problems can be a very painful experience. I know this because I was required to complete a moral inventory as part of the addiction's recovery process. Up until that point I had blamed my problems on the government in the same way some people in the United States blame the deep state and cabals of paedophiles for theirs. When I really thought about why I blamed the government for my problems, I was unable to define the specific part of the government that was causing my alcoholism, making me act like an ass, or holding me back from the employment I felt I deserved with little education, or training. It was only when I stopped blaming others, grew up and took responsibility for my behaviour that I began to grow. Was it fun? No, absolutely not, and at times I felt tremendous shame and guilt around my drunken behaviour and the impact it had had on others. In spite of this, it was a process that caused rapid emotional growth. Introspection is the key to growth. Blaming is the key to emotional stagnation.

My point being that in the same way humans like to distract themselves from their problems, and dealing with them, the government acts in the same way. The key to addressing the governments in the United States and Canada's legitimacy to govern issue is for the governments to look internally and see why the public has so little respect for them. The government needs to look beyond who did what in the January 6 insurrection in Washington and the truck convoy in Ottawa and ask why the government, and government employees like the police, were treated with so little respect. In the Ottawa truck convoy situation, the problem was not solved for two, or three weeks in spite of government directives and a plea from the Prime Minister. It clearly seems that people are less compliant and will no longer readily do as the government tells and advises them to do. This has huge implications as the number of people who hold contempt for the government increases. If there was a war would the country pull together, or would there be half who refuse to defend the country? If there are major natural disasters can those who are politically, racially and economically divided come together in a group effort? If not, we have a massive problem. We see this with the situation where Russia has senselessly attacked Ukraine. Some United States present and former politicians, like Donald Trump have come out in support of Russia. This is an absolute disgrace but it shows that divisions run deep and when there is a crisis it is unknown how the country will respond. Twenty years ago, there would have been a united front to major problems, without question. The same thing happened with Trump's attacks on allies and his wanting the United States to go it alone. One can only hope that with the Ukraine situation he now has the intelligence to have figured out the value of NATO. I am sure he has but his love of Putin leads me to wonder what would happen if he were re-elected in 2024.

There is not just a national political divide in the United States but the Republican Party has a massive divide within it that is doing a great deal of damage to the party's fortunes because people do not know who represents the party; some level-headed, intelligent Republican, or some far-right zealot who has a big mouth but achieves nothing. People may like their local Republican candidate but they have to consider whether or not they would like Boebert, Taylor-Greene, Cawthorn, Jordon and people like McCarthy and Cruz to have more power when they have severely abused that which they have. No thank you!

The question needing to be answered is how can the United States and Canada restore faith in their governments? How can they regain the trust and respect of the citizenry? Why has this respect and faith in government been lost and what actions within the government caused this? There needs to be a plan to identify the sources of the problem and an incremental plan needs to be developed in response to it, in order to restore faith in each government. Like the moral inventory I did, the government will see a pattern of problems and abuses that led to the situation we see today. The process will be painful at times and unfortunately some individuals who have become the poster children for abuses cannot be eliminated because they are elected officials. The voters need to take care of the Gosar's and Taylor-Greene's of the world. On a daily basis, without shame or remorse they damage the United States democracy and spew their white supremacist hate and make hugely divisive comments to gain attention. This self-centredness and childish attention seeking has been allowed by Kevin

McCarthy, a Trump sycophant, and few Republicans have the backbone to stand up to Trump even when he puts personal revenge ahead of party interests.

It is quite ironic that the Canadian Government was quite happy to have $750,000 and $1,000,000 fines for those who violated the Covid-19 quarantine rules yet the Prime Minister got caught for two major ethical violations and there was no consequence. Perhaps this speaks to the problem. Obviously, since there was no deterrent and penalty, the Prime Minister saw fit to commit another ethical violation after the first. There must be legal consequences and progressive discipline to deal with politicians like this. The Prime Minister obviously feels that the Covid-19 fines were appropriate, yet the government will not do anything to create serious consequences for serious breaches of trust and ethical and legal violations. Obviously, this breeds contempt for the government and those who violate the rules, and unlike us, have no consequence.

Perception is reality and in the United States the Supreme Court is suspected of being partisan, despite claims by some justices that it is not. Recent findings about Clarence Thomas' wife and her attendance at the January 6 insurrection, and belief in conspiracy theories has brought the courts objectivity into question. Clarence Thomas voting record always struck me as odd because without fail he supports right-wing issues. In a recent case all justices other than Thomas voted one way and he another.

- Clarence Thomas' wife Ginni reportedly texted Mark Meadows urging him to overturn the 2020 election.

- The news prompted scrutiny on Thomas' lone dissent in a ruling rejecting Trump's bid to withhold docs from the Jan. 6 House panel.

- The New York Times previously reported that Ginni Thomas had ties to organizers of the Jan. 6 rally, which she has denied.

In January, the Supreme Court rejected former President Donald Trump's bid to block the release of some presidential records to the House committee investigating the Capitol riot in a near unanimous 8-1 vote.

Only one justice dissented: Clarence Thomas.

At the time, the justice provided no explanation for why he would have approved

Trump's request — a standard omission when the top court addresses emergency motions.

But Thomas' objection fell under scrutiny on Thursday after The Washington Post reported that the justice's wife, Virginia "Ginni" Thomas, sent multiple text messages to former White House chief of Staff Mark Meadows urging him to overturn the 2020 presidential election in the aftermath of Trump's loss to President Joe Biden.[27]

Interesting how Justice Thomas did not see fit to recuse himself from the deliberations around the release of these documents. Whether Thomas thought he was being objective or not, the fact that his wife exchanged numerous emails with White House insider Mark Meadows, asking him to overturn the election results should have resulted in Justice Thomas recusing himself. This has hurt the credibility of the Supreme Court and adds fuel to claim that the court is highly partisan. If perception is as important as reality, the Supreme Court appears

---

27   Business Inside-Mexico. *Clarence Thomas was the lone dissent In the Supreme Court's January order rejecting Donald Trump's bid to withhold documents from the January 6 panel.* March 24, 2022.

to have one member who is clearly partisan and has almost always voted accordingly it seems. The whole Supreme Court lacks credibility at this point and the only way for the court to regain credibility would be if Justice Thomas resigns. I very much doubt he will though and so the Supreme Court will not have the credibility and appearance of objectivity and fairness that it should have.

> Ginni Thomas is entitled to her opinions, but the issue for Justice Thomas is whether he should have recused himself from cases relating to the election and the Capitol riot on January 6, 2021, Williams noted.

> "In February 2021, Justice Thomas wrote a dissent after the majority declined to hear a case filed by Pennsylvania Republicans that sought to disqualify certain mail-in ballots. In January 2022, Thomas was the only justice who said publicly that he was against allowing the release of records from the Trump White House related to the Jan. 6 attack ... the glaring appearance of a conflict is more than enough to justify Justice Thomas's stepping aside from all matters related to January 6."

If Thomas doesn't recuse himself from participating in January 6-related cases, Williams argued, no one "should be shocked that America has lost faith in its highest court." (Justice Thomas returned home Friday after a week long hospital stay for what a court spokesman described as an infection.)[28]

It is difficult for any organization to maintain credibility when it is perceived to have someone who has involved themselves in what appears to be a blatant conflict of interest and who has chosen not to recuse themselves when legal analysts generally say they should have. When you have an undemocratic political system and a Supreme Court that appears to lack impartiality, is it any wonder people have increasingly less trust in the government? Political nonsense, lies and misinformation are one thing, but the Supreme Court is critical to protecting the citizenry from abuses by politicians and to protecting the Constitution. Government corruption and the legitimacy of governments extends well beyond those who are elected to hold office. Corrupt bureaucracies

---

28   Richard Galant. CNN Opinion. *The texts that shook the Supreme Court.* March 27, 2022.

can also do tremendous damage, intentionally, or unintentionally to the credibility of governments. One example, of this would be the bureaucrat who prepares a briefing note for a Minister, or other elected official that is not truthful, or distorts the truth to a point where other politicians and the media take the politician who used the briefing note to task for lying, when they had no choice but to rely on a bureaucrat to prepare a briefing note on the issue. This is because no Minister is aware of everything that happens within their portfolio. A bureaucrat of one political stripe can set up a politician of another to look bad. It is easy to do and can cost a politician dearly.

As I write this book, I am thinking that rather than asking why people do not trust the government, we should be asking why in the world would they? If the government wishes to regain our trust, it needs to take a good hard look at the type of abuses and corruption that are happening and develop a plan to clean them up. This would involve developing serious consequences for financial and ethical abuses and abuses of democracy and the Constitution. Violations of one's oath of office should also result in severe consequences. The lack of rules and consequences for abuses is appalling and as each day passes, we wonder if Trump and other politicians involved in the January

6 insurrection will be held to legally account for their actions. I have little confidence that much of anything will happen because each legal decision can be appealed until they get to the Supreme Court and it can no longer be counted on to be impartial, fair and non-partisan.

The Party With No Platform

Most people want to vote for a candidate based on what they perceive as the candidates' assets, and the platform of the party they represent. Unfortunately, many elections nowadays offer little in the way of ideas but a great deal in terms of smearing opponents and catering to racists, those who believe misinformation and conspiracy theories, and those who feel they have somehow been wronged by the state. Smearing an opponent says more about the person doing the smearing than the person who is being smeared. Politics have become entertainment, rather than the means through which we select the most qualified people to represent us. As a result, we often end up with people who have been professional entertainers, like Ronald Reagan, Jessie "The Body" Ventura and Arnold Schwarzenegger to name but a few. Image is more important than substance and there is little offered to the critical thinker, who is more interested in substance than image. Lies, allegations and what should be irrelevant information in terms of someone's ability to govern, all come into the political circus which is more commonly referred to as an election campaign. For example, Trump's allegations about Hunter Biden, have never been proven to have any substance and are irrelevant to Joe Biden's ability to be the President of the United States. If our kids make mistakes, which many kids do, does this mean that their parents should be disqualified from certain jobs? I hope not or, many people should not be working, whose kids have made mistakes, but who are exceptional at performing the duties of their jobs.

The media latches onto some irrelevant story and without any substantiation of wrongdoing goes on and on about it. Hunter Biden is not in politics yet he has been accused repeatedly of wrongdoing in Ukraine. I wish he would have the people and media perpetuating the myth that he has done something wrong charged with defamation of character if there is no truth to their allegations. The other thing that happens, is that while we are hearing everything about Hunter Biden's alleged wrongdoings, we are not hearing about information that may assist us in making informed electoral choices. If we want better political candidates, we need to force them to tell us what they will do and what their party platform is, if they have one, and are not a member of the Trump party. The Republican party used to have a platform but that has gone by the wayside, Whatever Trump says is where the party stands on issues and there is no platform. I imagine things could get very nasty if the Republican party did try to hammer out a platform because it is a deeply divided party.

Trump seems to view Putin as the source of truth we should all listen to. No thank you. It is telling that Trump feels he must seek Putin's assistance to verify his comments, although both lack credibility and Trump is a chronic liar as evidenced by the 30,000+ lies he told when he was the President. I can see why Trump would feel that he needs to verify his comments because otherwise we just assume he has lied again.

During the last United States election, I found myself asking what the Republican Party platform was. What was the plan? What ideas did the party have around the major issues confronting the United States? I am not a Republican but was waiting to hear what good ideas the Republicans may put forward. There were no ideas and there was no platform. I think people are expected to vote in lieu of any ideas and a Republican party platform because the great Donald

Trump is in charge and U.S. citizens should blindly follow him no matter how he conducts himself. This is because Trump is a narcissist and he thinks he is smarter than everyone else and people should follow him and recognize his superiority and brilliance. Surprisingly, in lieu of any platform about 70 million United States citizens voted for Donald Trump. I think the voters liked the idea that Trump perceived himself as a victim in the same way they did. He claimed to be tired of the government operating in the same old ways it always had and the voters bought this. Perhaps the voters felt that they too were victims of various abuses and that Trump was the first candidate that was in the same boat they were. He would champion their causes and stop the greed in Washington, and the ongoing persecution of the public by the left. He basically asked the public to buy into his narcissism and delusions and they did so completely. This was tremendously ironic because Trump is a member of the group that has made his wealth on the backs of the people who could hardly wait to support him.

> The Republican party has no platform per se because there have been no new inclusions since the last one that the party used.

The Republican Party took an unusual approach to writing its convention platform for 2020: It decided not to write one.

Rather, the GOP is reusing its platform from four years ago, which was written before Donald Trump became president. That means Republican delegates will not go through the usual process of deliberating over policies and principles to determine what the party stands for in 2020, as Democrats recently did.

A Republican National Committee (RNC) resolution on the topic says the reason the party has no new platform is the Covid-19 pandemic, which has necessitated a scaled-back convention this year. Since all the delegates couldn't gather in person, they claim, they're not doing a platform.

But that's not all there is to the story. Just a few months ago, word leaked out that Trump's team, led by his son-in-law and senior adviser Jared Kushner, had big plans to shake up the platform by dramatically shortening it — plans that drew the ire of some conservative activists, who were used to exerting their influence on the lengthy document.

So, back in June, the party made the decision to skip platform-drafting entirely and just reuse the 2016 document, citing the pandemic as the reason. It's unclear if this was done deliberately to avoid messy party infighting over the platform, but it certainly had that effect.

After all, it would have been possible to draft a platform virtually; Democrats just did so. Republicans weren't prevented from doing the same, but they chose not to bother. Instead of policy, the RNC's brief resolution on the topic repeatedly cites one major organizing principle that the Republican Party will adhere to for the next four years: support of President Trump.[29]

So, the message is that people should just trust Donald Trump's leadership and not question what the party is doing, or has planned should Trump be re-elected. This is the blind faith approach and it is

---

29   Andrew Prokop. Vox. *Why Republicans didn't write a platform for their convention this year.* August 24, 2020.

quite surprising it has been accepted given long-term politicians like Mitch McConnell, who for thirty years have always been part of a party with a party platform. Rather than thinking about the inner workings of the party, the party should have considered that for many a party platform is an expectation, and so it should be. A party platform lets voters know what to expect from a party and creates something that the party can later be measured against in the future. There is no party accountability without one. I would not vote for a party that refused to tell me its plan if elected. Nor would I want to engage with an organization that, like a cult, has put its faith in a leader and has scrapped its ideas and anything that does not support the leader's whims and desires. Quite pathetic for a group of politically experienced adults who at times over the period Trump has been involved with the party appear to have no backbone, or ability to think independently. Perhaps they are too fearful of the bully to express their thoughts. The party must feel that Trump can win the next election but that is questionable, and particularly since he has cozied up to Vladimir Putin since Russia attacked Ukraine. What is problematic for the Democrats is that Joe Biden is not a popular president and this increases Trump's chances of winning an election if he is not in jail for the numerous charges he is presently facing.

INSURRECTION

These cases charge Trump for his role in the January 6 2021 insurrection. Two allege that he undermined the counting of the electoral college votes. The rest accuse him of inciting the riots which caused physical and emotional harm to police officers.

DC attorney general investigating Trump over January 6 riots

Karl Racine is investigating Trump's potential role in encouraging the January 6 riots, though no charges have been filed.

- DC Attorney General: Prosecutors Could Charge Trump with Misdemeanor over Capitol Riots

Criminal

Pending

Congresspeople suing Trump over Capitol attacks

Eleven members of the US House are suing Trump, his personal attorney Rudy Giuliani and two militia groups – the Oath Keepers and Proud Boys – for conspiring to incite the violence at the Capitol.

- Ten more members of Congress join NAACP lawsuit against Trump and Giuliani for conspiring to incite US Capitol riot

Civil

Pending

Representative Swalwell suing Trump and others for Capitol riots

Eric Swalwell is suing Trump and others for allegedly inciting the violence at the Capitol building.

- The man who sued Trump for incitement: Politics Weekly Extra

Civil

Pending

Seven Capitol police officers sue Trump

Seven Capitol police officers who say they were injured physically or emotionally during the insurrection are accusing Trump and others of intentionally inciting the attack. Trump has filed a motion to dismiss the case.

- Capitol police officers sue Trump and far-right groups over 6 January attack

Civil

Pending

Two Capitol police officers sue Trump

Two Capitol police officers who were injured during the insurrection are accusing Trump of inciting the attack and suing him for the harm they suffered. Trump has filed a motion to dismiss the case.

- Police officers sue Donald Trump for injuries resulting from Capitol riot

Civil

Pending

Two police officers sue Trump over Capitol riot

Two DC metro officers accuse Trump of directing and inciting the riot that led to them being assaulted by poles and pepper spray.

- Three more police officers sue Trump over 6 January attack

Civil

Pending

Capitol police officer sues Trump over January 6 riot

Marcus J Moore is suing Trump for his role in the January 6 riot. The lawsuit says Trump allegedly "inflamed, encouraged, incited, directed" the insurrectionist mob, causing Moore and other officers to suffer injuries.

- Another US Capitol Police officer sues Trump for damages from Jan. 6

Civil
Pending

FINANCIAL

Trump is facing several lawsuits and criminal investigations into possible financial improprieties. Most of these cases allege that he lied or misled the government to reduce the amount of taxes he and his company paid.

Criminal investigation into finances

Manhattan prosecutors are investigating Trump and his company for potential financial and tax crimes, as well as insurance fraud. The Trump Organization has already been charged with giving employees perks without paying taxes on them.

- Trump's longtime accountant testifies to NY grand jury in criminal probe

Criminal

Pending

Westchester golf course investigation

The district attorney's office in Westchester, New York, is investigating Trump's golf course in the county, reportedly homing in on whether the Trump Organization underreported property values to reduce its tax liability.

- Trump Organization, Already Under Indictment, Faces New Criminal Inquiry

Criminal

Pending

New York state attorney general investigates Trump Organization for fraud

Letitia James is investigating Trump's company for allegedly manipulating the valuations of his real estate properties, and in turn avoiding tax liabilities. The investigation is looking into civil and criminal matters. Trump has sued James targeting him for political reasons.

- New York attorney general vows Trump investigation will proceed 'undeterred'

Civil

Pending

Misuse of 2017 inauguration money

The Washington DC attorney general is accusing Trump's 2017 inauguration committee of misusing assets to profit the Trump family. An earlier allegation that the committee made improper payments to Trump's DC hotel was dismissed by a judge.

- Ivanka Trump quizzed as part of inauguration fund lawsuit

Civil

Pending

Mary Trump fraud suit

Mary Trump, Donald Trump's niece, is suing him and his siblings for allegedly defrauding her out of inheritance money. Trump has moved to dismiss the lawsuit, with a decision pending.

- Mary Trump sues president and two of his siblings over fraud allegations

Civil

Pending

Trump Corporation class-action suit

An anonymous group of plaintiffs accused Trump, three of his children and his company of misleading people to invest in bogus business opportunities. It was later revealed Trump was a paid spokesperson for one of those companies which was featured on The Celebrity Apprentice.

- The lawsuit

Civil

Pending

ELECTION INTERFERENCE

Trump faces two lawsuits tied to his alleged efforts to interfere with the 2020 election. The Georgia case is a criminal investigation.

Fulton county election interference investigation

The district attorney's office in Fulton county, Georgia, is investigating whether Trump interfered with the election by trying to pressure Georgia secretary of state Brad Raffensperger to overturn the results in a recorded phone call. On the call, Trump told Raffensperger, "I just want to find 11,780 votes" – the precise number he needed to win.

- Georgia prosecutor seeks special grand jury into Trump's election interference

Criminal
Pending

NAACP sues Trump and RNC for trying to overturn election results

Local voters in Detroit are suing Trump and the Republican National Committee for threatening to overturn the election results in Michigan, arguing that the move would have disenfranchised Black voters in Wayne county. Trump has filed a motion to dismiss the case.

- Trump Accused in Suit of 'Pressure' to Undo Michigan Vote

Civil

Pending

SEXUAL MISCONDUCT

Trump has faced several accusations of sexual misconduct since he was elected president. One was a civil suit filed by former Apprentice contestant Summer Zervos who accused Trump of defamation after he said her allegations of sexually inappropriate behavior were a part of the Clinton's campaign's efforts to smear him. Zervos dropped the lawsuit in late 2021, but a similar defamation case is still ongoing.

E Jean Carroll defamation suit

Carroll has accused Trump of raping her at a New York department store in the 1990s. In response, Trump accused Carroll of lying, saying she was "not my type". Carroll is suing Trump for defamation. Trump has tried to get the case dismissed.

- Trump lawyers argue US government should take his place in E Jean Carroll lawsuit

Civil
Pending

OTHER

Trump is facing two other lawsuits related to the alleged actions of individuals who recently worked for him.

Former top Ukraine adviser sues Trump for retaliation

Retired Lt Col Alexander Vindman, a former top Ukraine expert in the Trump administration who testified to Congress during Trump's first impeachment, is suing Trump and several allies for allegedly retaliating against him.

- Retired Lt. Col. Alexander Vindman files federal lawsuit accusing Trump and Rudy Giuliani of violating the Ku Klux Klan Act

Civil
Pending

Trump Tower assault suit

Six protesters are suing Trump after his then head of security, Keith Schiller, allegedly assaulted them during a demonstration outside Trump Tower in 2015. Trump gave a deposition for this case in October 2021.

- Trump to testify in lawsuit by protesters who say guard assaulted them in 2015

Civil
Pending

Michael Cohen suit

Trump's former personal attorney, Michael Cohen, is accusing Trump and the US government of sending him back to prison as a retaliatory measure after Cohen wrote a tell-all memoir about his work for Trump.

- Michael Cohen sues Trump claiming retaliatory imprisonment[30]

It is important to make a distinction between civil and criminal cases. Civil cases can have quite severe penalties but do not result in the accused going

---

30   Guardian U.S. Staff. *The long list of legal cases against Donald Trump.* February 7, 2022.

to jail if convicted. Criminal cases can result in the accused going to jail if convicted. Both types of cases can put someone in a very bad light, although Trump's abhorrent behaviour and criminality have seldom resulted in him being held fully accountable. It is difficult to understand why the Department of Justice has not charged Donald Trump with more crimes related to his attempted overturning of the United States election. Clearly, there is criminal behaviour involved and the committee investigating the January 6 insurrection has uncovered a number of illegal acts but still the Department of Justice has failed to act. The committee investigating the U.S. election does not have the power to lay charges against Donald Trump or anyone else, unfortunately. Given the criminal charges that may be laid and that he may be convicted for, it is unclear if Donald Trump will be in a position to run for president in 2024. If he does gain the presidency, he will then become immune to prosecution again, and that may very well be his primary motivation for running for the presidency.

The power of the whole party has been given to Donald Trump, despite him potentially being convicted in a number of civil suits and criminal cases. It is difficult to understand why the party would give all its power to a man who may be headed to jail. It is clear to many people that Donald Trump is not fit to lead a political party, let alone be president of the United States. Then there are those who excuse all the sexual abuse, criminal activity, shady business dealings and a whole lot more. They feel he is unquestionably the right person to lead the country and there is nothing that will lead them to believe otherwise. The vast majority of white evangelicals, QAnon members and members of right-wing white supremacist organizations support Trump without question. They see him as a man that can advance their agendas and he did just that for the evangelicals when he appointed a right-wing Supreme Court justice, when given the opportunity. Trump's relationships are all transactional so it is reasonable to conclude that he expected that a judge he appointed would support his positions on legal matters, like overturning the election, no matter how ludicrous. By appointing a right-wing judge, it became more likely that issues like abortion would be reconsidered and the laws changed in ways that would make evangelicals happy. This speaks in part to why the United States is no longer a democracy. The evangelicals may be happy but the majority may not be. Catering to minority groups like the evangelicals is a risky gamble. By trying to secure the evangelical vote a greater number of votes from other Republicans may be lost.

Parties without platforms are able to do whatever they want, any time, to capitalize on politically expedient opportunities. The problem is that they appear to stand for nothing. The fact the party does not have a current party platform and is divided on whether Russia should be supported, in spite of its unprovoked attack on Ukraine, gives me no reason to think the party is a) united, b) has positions on anything and, c) is not anti-democracy and pro white supremacy. Not a desirable combination and of no appeal to many.

Just the Facts

The media seems to feel the need to tell us the "news", and then tell us how we are supposed to view this information, feel about it, and emotionally respond to it. Facebook uses algorithms to ensure that we are fed information that is consistent with our political views, leading us to believe that everyone thinks as we do and that there should be a landslide victory for the political party we support. I never receive right-wing perspectives and this is unfortunate because if I did, I would, a) understand the views of these people better, and b) may change some of my opinions based on new information. Is it any wonder the United States is so deeply divided when all anyone gets on Facebook are views consistent with their left-wing, or right-wing orientation? Fox News is a joke and is right-wing entertainment. CNN is left-wing. There is no need to classify all the media as left, or right-wing but there has been a move by many Fox viewers to view more hardcore right-wing media. The problem Fox now has, after allowing the spread of misinformation and lies via its hosts and guests, is that, if the hosts now tell the truth they will be seen to not be supporting the Republican party, or Donald Trump and Trump supporters will go elsewhere for their "news".

Having someone like Tucker Carlson, from Fox "News" provide a commentary on the news is laughable because he is a white supremacist and just not very smart. We would be far better to be given the facts and then apply critical thinking to them, than to have someone with no credibility like Carlson telling us how we should think about the information, or misinformation he has provided. If Tucker Carlson was intelligent, his analysis of the news may be of interest, but he is not, and his take on the news is extremely biased, and many of his conclusions make no sense. Apparently, there are many who lap up his nonsense and buy into his divisive rhetoric and propaganda. This may contribute to eventually destroying the country, and the democratic remnants of an earlier time that still remain.

A question that I asked in an earlier book that still seems relevant, is what happens when the vast majority of the population believes in a reality based on the one put forth by groups like QAnon, which includes misinformation and conspiracy theories too numerous to mention. People, who despite over sixty lawsuits that showed that the presidential election was not fraudulent still choose to believe it was. Is reality whatever the majority thinks it is? If so, we are in a lot of trouble in North America! Some media have been complicit in spreading misinformation about Joe Biden not winning the election fairly, about Covid-19 vaccines, about conspiracy theories, the deep state and other unidentifiable organizations.

Vaccines were politicized via the media and people like Donald Trump and so the factual information got lost and thousands died as a result. It was not enough for some media to simply give us the public health information we needed to make informed choices. No, Fox had to have guests on that made some fearful of getting vaccinated, while President Trump was holding super-spreader rallies with little, if any social distancing, no masks and no requirement that participants be vaccinated. It was as if being irresponsible and putting one's life at risk showed allegiance to Donald Trump. Many people did die and this seemed to have no effect on Trump as he continued his super-spreader rallies and still continues them today. Since they are attended by Trump supporters one can only assume that they are held to give Trump the external validation he requires, because he internally is a weak man who continually needs to be propped up by others.

In a world that is characterized by deep chasms most of the world's leaders realize that alliances are critical to the security of their countries. Donald Trump had no use for the North Atlantic Treaty Organization (NATO) and failed to see the value in it. Whether this was because not supporting NATO played into Putin's hands, or for some other reason is unclear. What is abundantly clear post Trump is that if NATO had been dismantled, Ukraine would have been obliterated weeks ago. This is all quite ironic because Trump praised Putin when the attack on the Ukraine by Russia was initiated, which makes me wonder how Trump's ongoing love of Putin may have had to do with his desire to disband NATO. A leader who puts the interests of another country before the interests of their own is not fit to govern. Thankfully, President Biden had the sense to re-establish alliances that former President Trump worked so hard at destroying. His idea that the United States could and should go it alone was both silly and dangerous. This is especially true since the leaders of China and Russia recently met and formed some sort of alliance, albeit an unclear one.

At this point Trump has major criminal issues but is still teasing a run at the Presidency in 2024. This is of obvious concern to NATO countries and others that would like a stable world, where offsetting powers keep all in check. We know Trump has wanted to put a hotel in Moscow and has relationships with some business people from Russia, so perhaps his support of Russia is for personal gain at the expense of the United States and its NATO alliances. When one understands that Donald Trump is self-serving and only seems to act out of self-interest the picture becomes much clearer. It is appalling that 70 million people wanted Trump to be the President of the United States in the last election. He is not fit to govern and never has been. This is being increasingly proven by the committee researching the events surrounding and leading to the attempted coup of January 6.

As we try to sort out for ourselves what is happening in the world and what it all means we are given completely different views by different sources of media.

> Those with consistently conservative political values are oriented around a single outlet—Fox News—to a much greater degree than those in any other ideological group: Nearly half (47%) of those who are consistently conservative name Fox News as their main source for government and political news. Far fewer choose any other single

source: Local radio ranks second, named by 11%, with no other individual source named by more than 5% of consistent conservatives. Those with mostly conservative views also gravitate strongly toward Fox News – 31% name it as their main source, several times the share who name the next most popular sources, including CNN (9%), local television (6%) and radio (6%) and Yahoo News (6%).

On the left of the political spectrum, no single outlet predominates. Among consistent liberals, CNN (15%), NPR (13%), MSNBC (12%) and the New York Times (10%) all rank near the top of the list. CNN is named by just 20% of those with mostly liberal views, but still tops their list, followed by local television (11%) and NPR (9%). Both MSNBC and Fox News are mentioned by 5% of those who are mostly liberal. Those in other ideological groups name the New York Times, NPR and MSNBC less frequently as top news sources.[31]

---

31 Amy Mitchell, Jeffery Gottfried, Jocelyn Kelly, Katrina Eva Matsa. *Pew Research Centre. Section 1: Media Sources: Distinct favourites emerge on the left and right.* October 21, 2014

We also know that social media companies use algorithms to tell us what we want to hear and what Facebook wants us to see, to generate profits from advertising.

What is the Facebook algorithm?

The Facebook algorithm determines which posts people see every time they check their Facebook feed, and in what order those posts show up.

Essentially, the Facebook algorithm evaluates every post. It scores posts and then arranges them in descending, non-chronological order of interest for each individual user. This process happens every time a user—and there are 2.9 billion of them— refreshes their feed.

We don't know all the details of how the Facebook algorithm decides what to show people (and what not to show people). But we do know that—like all social media rec- ommendation algorithms—one of its goals is to keep people on the platform, so that they see more ads.

In fact, Facebook faced heat in 2021 because the algorithm was prioritizing controversial content. Controversy often gets the highest engagement and can even trigger "compulsive use" of the platform.

And as far back as 2018, critics feared the algorithm was increasing outrage, divisiveness and political polarization while promoting misinformation and borderline content.[32]

Obviously, algorithms do not promote a realistic and objective view of the world. We as viewers are confronted with politically biased media and social media that uses algorithms that harm society. Given this, it should not have surprised me when I have travelled, that the world is very different from the skewed version we receive via North American media. This is in part because "controlling the narrative" can be politically expedient and hugely profitable. Reality falls somewhere below profits, advertising exposure and ratings when the priorities of media outlets of various sorts are considered. It is not real and do we really want a twit like Tucker Carlson telling us how

---

32   Chris Newberry. Hootsuite. *How the facebook algorithm works in 2022 and how to make it work for you.* February 28, 2022.

we should think about the news when he seems largely incapable of rational thought? Do we want some left-wing zealot sensationalizing events to increase ratings? No, we just want what we so seldom seem to get anymore and that is just the facts. The viewer is quite capable of drawing their own conclusions and do not need justifications for political corruption, sexual abuse, misogyny, racism or other forms of hate in its many forms. Just the damn facts, please!

Incompetence, Discontent and Rise of the Right

R ight-wing politics taken to their extreme are scary, as evidenced by Hitler and the Nazis in Second World War Germany. We are presently seeing the rise of the right in many countries and populism, although increasingly popular, has proven to be the poorest form of government when confronted with a national emergency like Covid-19. I think this is because populist governments tend to get elected when there is a wave of dissatisfaction with the status quo and the momentum of a charismatic leader. Populism is about image and this is not necessarily accompanied by substance. Just because there is general dissatisfaction with the status quo does not mean that any change in governance will represent an improvement. Nor does it mean that the new leader has competence, or the ability to handle emergencies of a national magnitude, as we saw in the United States, Brazil and

India. The media and governments tend to portray the rise of the right in many countries as a surprise. I would argue that it should come as absolutely no surprise and that governments are generally not willing to do what needs to be done to restore confidence in democratic governments in the countries that have them.

If you have tired of the corruption, transactional politics, politicians paying the electorate lip service and kowtowing to lobby groups and corporations you may be looking for a party that represents a radical change in ideology. Perhaps you are tired of seeing politicians committing ethical violations with no consequence and are tired of your leader embarrassing your country by playing Mr. Costumes and calling elections for no reason other than personal ego. Elections that cost $600 million and that essentially resulted in the same minority government. Perhaps you are tired of your Congressperson and Senator being bought and paid for by lobby groups and corporations. Perhaps, you see voting as being little more than a carrot given to people so that they are deluded into thinking that they are being represented, in an attempt to appease them. Above all else, the unwillingness to improve the system and protect democracy and the Constitution is avoided by politicians because it may result in fewer personal goodies and a potential loss of power. If governments want to know why the right has been rising rapidly in many countries, they need do nothing more than look internally at the ongoing abuses that are now systemic in nature and are ingrained in the political systems in North America. The question should not be why the right is rising rapidly, but should be why present governments are not working to strengthen democracies and why harsher measures are not taken to deal with corruption of the magnitude both Trump and Trudeau have engaged in. Why would people not be looking for an alternative? The answers are internal but I do not believe the Canadian government, or the U.S. Senate and Congress will look internally with the intent of fixing a badly flawed system that is all about money and power and not much else. The pathetic gun violence responses result from fear that if the politician votes to bring guns under control, they will have less money for their next campaign when the gun lobby cuts them off. Anyone can see the system is flawed.

People who like the government simply are not paying attention, or feel that severe corruption in both the Canadian and American political systems is just part of doing business and is acceptable. How does a politician who is a salesperson get elected for four years and then become a millionaire? Can someone explain to me how that happens? Why can the Prime Minister have two major, blatantly obvious ethical violations and still be Prime Minister and why in the world would anyone trust him? His apologies mean nothing when after the first apology there is more blatantly unethical conduct, as identified by the Ethics Commissioner.

What has the consequence been? None that I am aware of and this from the same man who wanted to levy extremely heavy-handed penalties out to those who violated Covid-19 rules. I think there should be a one strike rule for severe ethical violations. There should also be criminal prosecution for politicians who break the law, rather than a slap on the wrist. The differential treatment given to politicians who break the law is another reason the public has little respect for the institution of government. Some young person goes to jail for two years for the theft of $2,000, while no one went to jail for the Sponsorship scandal, the WE fiasco, or a host of other things. That reminds me with respect to the WE debacle. If you were to do what is outlined below do you think the police would have charged you and that you would have been prosecuted? Again, just for reference the situation involved the Liberal party that has been so heavy-handed with

Canadians around Covid-19 and they have never even broken the law. Do differential rules for politicians breed contempt among the public? Remember that without good reason government contracts must go to tender and cannot be sole-sourced.

A time-line of events regarding the $912-million Canada Student Service Grant program, based on public events and statements from cabinet ministers, government officials, and WE Charity:

April 5: Finance Minister Bill Morneau and Prime Minister Justin Trudeau talk over the phone about how to help students whose summer job and volunteer opportunities were vanishing due to the Covid-19 pandemic. Finance Department officials are tasked with considering options the next morning.

April 7: Morneau's office contacts the WE organization, among other groups, to get their input on potential programs.

April 9: WE Charity sends an unsolicited proposal for a youth entrepreneurship program to Morneau, Youth Minister Bardish Chagger, Small Business Minister Mary

Ng and Trudeau's office. The price tag is between $6 million and $14 million, and the proposal is to provide digital programming and $500 grants, plus "incentive funds," for 8,000 students.

April 16: Employment and Social Development Canada officials mention WE in the context of the student program in an email discussion with Finance Department officials.

April 18: Morneau's officials raise the idea of partnering with a non-profit or for-profit group to administer the program. (ESDC officials suggest the same day that WE might be an option.) Morneau said it was the first time he was involved in any talk about WE and the grant program.

How to re-watch this week's hearings on the WE contract controversy

April 19: A senior official at Employment and Social Development Canada, Rachel Wernick, contacts WE co-founder Craig Kielburger. She learns of the April 9 proposal.

April 20: Morneau's office contacts WE to ask about its ability to deliver a volunteer program. An official's record of the call notes "WE Charity will re-work their 10-week summer program proposal to fully meet the policy objective of national service and increase their current placements of 8,000 to double."

April 21: Morneau approves going with an outside organization to run the volunteer program, but no specific group is chosen.

April 22: Trudeau announces a $9-billion package of student aid which includes the outline of a volunteer program paying students up to $5,000 toward education costs, based on the number of hours they volunteer. WE sends Wernick an updated proposal to reflect the announcement.

April 26: Morneau speaks with WE co-founder Craig Kielburger — but later told the finance committee neither of them talked about the Canada Student Service Grant program.

May 4: WE sends a third proposal to Employment and Social Development Canada, this time with more details specific to the grant program. Finance Department official Michelle Kovacevic, who was working on the program, told the finance committee she received it May 7.

May 5: Chagger goes to a special Covid-19 cabinet committee with the recommendation to go with WE for the program. Morneau isn't at the meeting.

Services Grant program to the WE Charity organization. (Adrian Wyld/Canadian Press)

May 22: Cabinet, including Trudeau and Morneau, approves handing the reins of the program to WE.

May 23: The public service officially begins negotiating a contribution agreement with WE, which would have paid up to $43.5 million in fees to the group.

May 25 to June 3: In a series of meetings with Volunteer Canada, WE suggests the target for placements through the program had gone from 20,000 to 100,000.

June 12: WE co-founder Marc Kielburger says in a video chat with youth leaders that he heard from Trudeau's office about getting involved in the volunteer program the day after it was announced by the prime minister. He later backtracks, saying the contact came the week of April 26 from Wernick, and not the PMO.

June 23: WE is informed the contribution agreement has been approved.

June 25: Trudeau unveils more details about student aid. A government release notes that WE will administer the student-volunteer program. **Trudeau says only**

June 26: Facing questions about WE, Trudeau says the non-partisan public service made the recommendation and the government accepted it: "As the public service dug into it, they came back with only one organization that was capable of networking and organizing and delivering this program on the scale that we needed it, and that was the WE program."

July 3: Citing the ongoing controversy, WE and the Liberals announce a parting of ways and the federal government takes control of the program. Ethics commissioner Mario Dion tells Conservative and NDP ethics critics in separate letters he will examine Trudeau's role in the awarding of the agreement because of the prime minister's close ties to the group.

July 9: WE says it has paid Trudeau's mother Margaret about $250,000 for 28 speaking appearances at WE-related events between 2016 and 2020. His brother Alexandre was paid $32,000 for eight events, and Trudeau's wife Sophie Gregoire Trudeau received $1,400 in 2012 for a single appearance. The organization says Trudeau himself has never been paid by the charity or its for-profit arm.[33]

You can draw your own conclusions as to whether or not this was a conflict of interest, or something worse. Appearance is as important as reality and anyone can see the problem here. It is precisely

---

33   CBC News-Politics. *A time-line of the WE charity controversy.* July 23, 2020.

this sort of ethical breach involving the Liberals that breeds contempt for the government.

The government has no one but itself to blame for the rise of the right. People are sick and tired of the ongoing political abuses, and so they should be. I cannot imagine Mr. Trudeau having the insight to look at his abuses in terms of what impact they have had on democracy and what they have done to people's general perception of national politics and government in general. It is a disgrace and with no insight and little desire to change a system that is corrupt by developing real consequences for politicians who violate public trust, nothing will change. There may be a change of government and the election of a party that falls on the extreme right of the political spectrum due to the actions of Trudeau, Morneau and countless other politicians over the years. This is because people will seek a radical departure from centrist and left-wing governments in response to the ongoing abuses. This is particularly true if the people have no viable left-wing, or centrist parties that could serve as an alternative to the corrupt one in power.

It is an illusion to think voting in an extreme right-wing party will solve a country's problems. This will not stop corruption, but when it gets to a point where it cannot get much worse, many voters may vote for a right-wing party. We are moving toward that point in both the United States and Canada, albeit, Canada more gradually than the U.S. It was this type of desperation to escape the status quo that led to Trump being elected. Desperation to clean up the corruption in Washington, or as some put it, "to drain the swamp". Instead of dealing with the corruption, U.S. citizens got heaping doses of racism, cozying up to dictators like Vladimir Putin, divisive politics, Covid-19 incompetence, transactional governance and the attempted coup of January 6. It was a "careful what you wish for" scenario and when the United States elected Trump, the voters got a break from the status quo but also got a great deal of corruption. Whether this represented an improvement over past governments is debatable. I think it was one of the worst, if not the worst government in United States history and I would put it in the same league as the Nixon government. It is historical political abuse that brings voters to the point where they think anything is better than what is presently in place. It is things like Trudeau's ongoing ethical abuses, the whole January 6 mess, the Sponsorship scandal, Watergate and hundreds, if not thousands of other abuses. There appears to be little desire by those in power to change anything, and why would they want too when the system serves the public horribly but the politicians very nicely?

When you compare Trump and Trudeau there are many differences but also some glaring similarities. They have in common a strong sense of entitlement, a sense of superiority and arrogance about them, will use whatever approach garners them political support and both lack ethics and a moral compass. Not exactly qualities one would associate with a good leader. As the right rises in North America and people on the political left and centre bemoan this fact, they should remember that it was governments like we have today, and over the years, that have brought us to the point we are at today. This did not just randomly happen, and nor will it just randomly happen in the future when there is a hard turn back to the left, after years of right-wing abuses. This is an incremental process and that is why I believe there is not more response to the move away from democracy. To stop this pendulum like swing back and forth along the political spectrum there will need to be a real effort to protect the Constitutions of Canada and the United States and reform the two political systems in such a way that they are about representing the constituent first, rather than self-interest, lobby groups and corporations. In the United States that means bringing in rules that will stop the buying of elections and politicians by those who can afford them. In Canada it will mean bringing in very stiff penalties for corruption, ethical violations and other abuses. These should include heavy fines, suspensions, and where appropriate disbarment. For all other abuses in both countries the police should be brought in to conduct legal investigations and charges should be laid if guilt is found. There should no longer be committees tasked to look into abuses that cannot levy consequences when the police have the ability to conduct investigations and lay charges.

The pandering to, and protection of politicians from criminal charges must go. If anything, the penalties for these people should be more severe when they are in positions of public trust. What consequences did Morneau and Trudeau receive for their ethical violations? Now ask yourself what would have happened if you had abused your employer's rules in a similar way. Yes, you would not have an employer now but Trudeau still does and Morneau paid back the money and has resigned with apparently no further penalty. How does that work? If you were caught with funds, you should not have and you simply pay them back, would you walk away unscathed legally? What do you think would happen if you went down to Canadian Tire and were caught trying to shoplift something? Do you think a chuckle, returning the item to the store security person and a statement like, "no harm, no foul" would result in the guard not calling the police? That compared to a similar scenario where over $41,000 was involved and paid back and then a resignation followed and the Minister walked away with no real legal consequence, unless there is an ongoing investigation that I am unaware of. The point being that this is precisely the type of thing that has created deep cynicism and a lack of trust and contempt for politicians and governments. It is why there are increasing voices that democracy is not working and a movement toward right-wing, dangerously extreme politics. Do you think the governments in North America will do what is required to improve the situation?

Government's Role in Law Enforcement

If you are wondering why the political system is being afforded ever less credibility, look no further than how measures have been taken to decrease legal accountability for bribery and extortion and how the Canadian Government has allowed money laundering to continue to a point where most young Canadians cannot afford a home, and the elderly had better start looking to jails and mental institutions when it comes to housing, they can afford on their meagre pension cheques. Firstly, let's look at how it is virtually impossible to hold a U.S. politician accountable, followed by the money laundering situation in Canada. Both speak to how government negligence has led to terrible situations that damage democracy, the institution of government and the reputations of these countries in the eyes of others.

But the power of money to get donors political access and influence has expanded with the whittling away of corruption laws. I believe that because of the Supreme Court's erosion of limits on many kinds of campaign contributions, our current means of financing campaigns has devolved into a form of legalized bribery. Donors pour money into races to get officials who will support their favoured goals.

When the officials deliver, the money keeps rolling in. One example: After passage of the tax bill in December, conservative billionaire Charles Koch and his wife gave nearly $500,000 to House Speaker Paul Ryan's PAC.

In my opinion, the Supreme Court majority's decisions on corruption have demonstrated little concern about the corrosive effect of the decisions on the public's faith in their government. In Citizens United v. Federal Election Commission in 2010, the court struck down limits imposed on corporations to make "independent expenditures" on behalf of candidates because they "do not give rise to corruption or the appearance of corruption."

According to Justice Anthony Kennedy's majority opinion, "the appearance of influence or access will not cause the electorate to lose faith in this democracy."

After years of the Supreme Court narrowing even minimal protections against public corruption, the U.S. now has a system where what looks like bribery and corruption to the public is, in most cases, not illegal. Our political leaders are no longer kept in line by federal corruption law. They do not need to worry that if they bend over backwards to accommodate a donor's wishes, it could spark a bribery charge.[34]

It is basically legal to buy politicians and elections and there is little that can be done about it until the law changes. This reduction in legal accountability for political crimes like bribery and extortion leaves the public wondering what a politician has to do to be charged and prosecuted. They know that if they were

---

34   Peter J. Henning. The Conversation. *It's getting harder to prosecute politicians for corruption*. February 16, 2018.

to do something half as bad, they would be off to jail. They continue to see politician after politician getting away with actions that would result in jail time for them. And these are the people who make the laws!

Is breaking the law a politically risky act for politicians and other public officials? The question is especially important in the context of legislators and high executive officials who, for reasons of immunity or otherwise, are not subject to formal legal sanctions when they break the law. In such contexts, we might think that various other repercussions would serve in the place of formal legal sanctions, such that violating the Constitution or the law would entail tangible political, reputational, and social risks. Yet a raft of examples suggests, albeit not definitively, that violating the law *qua* law is not ordinarily subject to nonlegal sanctions. The electorate, the media, and most other potential sources of social and political sanctions reward good policy choices and sanction bad ones, but the very fact of illegality, except possibly by increasing the sanctions for bad policy choices that are also illegal, appears to play at most a small role in constraining the choices of a large group of the most influential and visible American public officials.[35]

So, the United States holds politicians, who are in positions of public trust to a lower standard of behaviour than the employee who works at the dump and a guy that flips hamburgers at a hamburger joint. How is that equality under the law as per the Constitution? It seems that the greater the position of public trust one is in, the less legal accountability they have. Should it not be the opposite? Since it is the government, through the various levels of policing and the courts that enforce the laws, should it not follow that those who work as politicians and who make the laws are held to the highest standards?

A lawmaker should not be a lawbreaker.

This maxim advises that a person who constitutes the law for others to follow should be the first person in following it and obeying it but he should not even try to alter to his needs and convenience or break or go beyond or against the law.

---

35   Frederick Schuaer. Journal of Legal Analysis, Volume 4, Issue 1, Spring 2012, Pages 83–101. *Political risks (if any) of breaking the law.* July 11, 2012.

Law is the one which makes the man behave sincerely. It makes the man to observe discipline and constrains him not to indulge in vice activities. A person who observes and obeys the law is an honest person. The behaviours of a lawmaker should be appreciable and should set an example to others. The teacher who insists punctuality should be punctual in his every act.

The politicians who amend laws in the constitution often bend them to their convenience. They often try to take advantage by breaking the law. They indulge in self-motive activities and sometimes they go beyond the law and dodge even the court of law. Those who amend laws should first abide by them. Otherwise, it would have a bad effect on society.[36]

As it is, there are rules that favour those who are responsible for creating the laws and who are in charge of those who enforce the law and prosecute those who break it? It is reasonable to think that if you are involved in politics, which involves creating and

---

36   English For Students. *A lawmaker should not be a lawbreaker.* Date of publication unspecified

passing laws, that you should serve as a role model for those who are expected to abide by the law. Rather than this we see blatant violations of trust, unethical, immoral and illegal behaviour and a system that provides all but immunity from prosecution. And then politicians wonder why many people are so cynical about politics and why the public is seemingly less willing to listen and abide by government directives. Covid-19 was a good example of this. It was clear many did not trust government advice about how to deal with the pandemic and chose not to get vaccinated. It was also obvious in Ottawa during the trucker anti-vaccination rules demonstration that many do not respect the government enough to listen to it. Sure, there were some right-wing elements involved but when truckers were asked to move their trucks many just ignored the government. You may think that this is no big deal but there are many crises where it is absolutely essential that people comply with government directives, or people can be injured, or die. I wonder if Trudeau would have felt the need to go and hide when the trucker convoy went to Ottawa if he had the respect of the public?

Who could possibly blame anyone who is not white for refusing to have a Covid-19 vaccine needle stuck in their arm, based on a recommendation by the government, after all the government abuses of minority groups over the years? In the case, of First Nations and Inuit in Canada where there seems to be an ongoing genocide taking place, it is a wonder that anyone would get vaccinated. After residential school abuse, the finding of graves of aboriginal children near residential schools across the country and years of other forms of horrible abuse, we cannot very well expect these folks to trust the government. They have every reason not to. The governments carry on as if nothing is wrong when it is clear that if they remain on the same trajectory, democracy will disappear, a civil war in the U.S. will ensue and anarchy will reign. Why? This is because of what the government and courts have allowed the government to become. It is corrupt, often about politicians, corporate and lobby group needs and the citizen is ignored. Oh sure, they are supposed to buy into the illusion that their vote makes a difference but how much does it really matter when politicians are being bought and sold like commodities. Allowing the public to vote is a measure of appeasement, and is apparently one the Republicans would just as soon not see continued. The January 6 coup being but one small example. The other being that Republicans will go to any lengths to retain white privilege and since people of colour are becoming a majority, Republicans see democracy as being problematic at this point.

A good example of how corruption can impact a country›s democracy and international reputation can be seen in the following passage.

> OTTAWA — Canada is still feeling the "ripple effect" of numerous recent political ethics and money laundering scandals as the country continues its "disappointing" drop to its lowest level ever on a global index of corruption. "The problem of money-laundering in Canada and other corruption scandals have been headline news in recent years dragging down the perception of Canada as a clean country. This year's disappointing results show the need to take concrete action to restore Canada's reputation," James Cohen, executive director of Transparency International (TI) Canada, said in a statement. Every year, the global corruption watchdog publishes a ranking of 180 countries based on their perceived levels of public-sector corruption. The Corruption Perception Index (CPI) aggregates data from up to 13 independent expert assessments to create a score for each country.

The scale goes from 0 (highly corrupt) to 100 (very clean). In 2021, Canada scored 74, good for 13th place on the scale but a drop of two compared to the previous year. That puts the country tied with Iceland, Ireland, Estonia and Austria but below many others including Denmark, Germany, Singapore and Hong Kong. Though Canada's rank is enviable compared to that of France (71) and the United States (67), it masks a concerning downward trend. The country's score has dropped 10 points since 2012. In fact, Transparency International notes that Canada is the country with the most significant drop in score of all 180 countries in the past five years. "I think Canadians are frustrated, and rightfully so," Cohen said in an interview. "What the public needs to do is keep up the pressure to make sure that changes come through." "We can't just rest on our image of Canada the good anymore, we need to see action." Cohen said there isn't a single incident or scandal that caused Canada's latest fall in the ranking. Rather, the country is likely feeling the shock waves of recent issues that have made worldwide headlines, namely ethics scandals involving the Trudeau government as well as the national reckoning of the scope of money laundering in Canada. "There's no there-there issue that made us drop, this is more about the ripple effect of what's happened over the last couple of years and not seeing a counterbalance in enforcement, new rules or the results of those new rules," Cohen said. He noted that since Justin Trudeau became head of Canada's government in 2015, he has been the target of three separate Ethics Commissioner investigations, two of which found that he had broken ethics laws. First came the prime minister's controversial vacation on the private island of billionaire philanthropist and leader of the Ismaili movement Aga Khan in 2017. Then Trudeau was found to have broken ethics laws again in 2019 in the SNC-Lavalin affair, when the commissioner found that he had improperly tried to pressure then-Justice Minister Jody Wilson-Raybould (who subsequently resigned) into brokering a remediation agreement with Canadian engineering giant SNC-Lavalin.

"We see in reports that the CPI is compiled from, this is obviously still on the mind of international observers," Cohen said. Cohen also noted the WE Charity scandal that rocked the Liberal government in 2020, leading to Finance Minister Bill Morneau's resignation and subsequent Ethics Commissioner ruling that he had breached the law. "It's not just the scandals, but it's also the lack of things that have been done," Cohen explained. "We've seen remediation agreements come into effect, but we have yet to see remediation agreements sealed, or finished." Then there's the reoccurring issue of money laundering in Canada, which has made headlines across the country, but particularly in British Columbia in recent years. Experts estimate that anywhere between $46 billion and $130 billion is laundered through Canada every year in a phenomenon billed "snow-washing." "Canada-wide, we need to see action on anti-money laundering. It's a national issue. And we need to see the federal government taking foreign bribery seriously too," Cohen said. But all is not lost for Canada. TI notes that the country has taken some important steps toward increased transparency as well as fighting corruption. But the results of those new initiatives are still to be seen. For example, the federal government as well as a few provinces have pledged to put in place a new beneficial ownership registry that would reveal the owners of shell corporations, which are often used in money laundering schemes in Canada. Cohen said he also hopes the Liberals go through with their election promise to create an anti-money laundering enforcement body. "For Canada to go back up, we need to start seeing the results of the good intentions," he concluded.[37].

Here we see the real impact on Canada when there is unethical conduct by the Prime Minister and others. Internationally Canada is being seen as a haven for money laundering and this has tarnished the country›s international reputation. Trudeau has done tremendous damage to the country through his failure to do much, if anything about money

---

37   Christopher Nardi. National Post. *Canada continues 'disappointing' drop in watchdog's global corruption index: report.* January 26, 2022.

laundering and through his two ethical violations and another allegation about unethical behaviour that he was exonerated for, but that sure looked like unethical conduct to most Canadians. What this means in real terms is that Canada has lost credibility internationally and when the Prime Minister talks about human rights abuses, democracy, the rule of law, ethical and moral conduct internationally he can be told that he needs to clean up his own backyard before pointing fingers at others. With residential school abuse, the abuse of the indigenous people, Japanese, Chinese and Black communities along with ongoing political corruption and massive money laundering, Canadians need to see the country for what it is and take off the rose-coloured glasses.

It will take time for Canada to restore its good international standing and that will only happen if the massive money laundering problem is addressed and if politicians like the Prime Minister stop acting like the leader of some sort of corrupt banana republic. Perhaps more alarming and upsetting than the corruption and abuses is how little has been done about them. What do you suppose a company would do if your behaviour put the company in a bad light internationally? Yes, you would be fired. If you were a politician, you may get a slap on the wrist and told you are a naughty boy, or girl and to not do it again. Then, like Trudeau, you could apologize and do it again, proving you were not sorry at all. Again, there would be no real consequence and therefore no deterrent to doing the same sort of thing repeatedly.

Since the Liberals have been in power for many years at this point it must be asked why there is such a massive money laundering problem in this country. Not only is money laundering a crime but it has also put the price of housing out of the reach of many Canadians. The Liberal Government is moving at a snail's pace to deal with this issue. It would not be surprising that when the government does deal with this issue that it may find many Russian oligarchs have money being laundered in Canada. Given the attack on Ukraine by Russia this issue needs to be addressed immediately and the dirty money owned by Russians must be dealt with in such a way that it cannot in any way be used to assist in funding this horrific attack on Ukraine. This is not a new issue and is hurting many Canadians. It is serving to tarnish Canada's international reputation, yet Trudeau has done virtually nothing about it since he was elected in 2015. It makes me wonder if there are people in high places laundering money who might surprise us and that are basically being protected through inaction on this issue. After seven years of money

laundering making housing unaffordable and stain-
ing Canada's international reputation you would have
thought this Liberal Government would have addressed
the issue. In a British Columbia report that talked about
the impact of money laundering on real estate, among
other things, it points out how money laundering is
helping to make housing unaffordable. I was not joking
when I suggested senior's on government pensions in
BC had better start looking at jail and mental institutions, as affordable housing if there are any mental
health facilities left after everyone was turfed out on
the street.

> Money laundering investment in BC real
> estate is sufficient to have raised housing
> prices and contributed to BC's housing
> affordability issue. The data limitations
> that make it difficult to estimate the level
> of money laundering make it even more
> challenging to estimate the allocation of
> money laundering to specific economic sec-
> tors, such as real estate and the impact of
> that investment on house prices. The Panel
> cautiously estimates that almost 5 percent
> of the value of real estate transactions in
> the province result from money laun-
> dering investment. The estimated impact

of that would be to increase housing prices by about 5 percent. Successfully reducing money laundering investment in BC real estate should have a modest but observable impact on housing affordability.[38]

The Government of British Columbia recognized the impact that money laundering has been having on real estate costs in BC and requested a review of this problem by three experts. This is what a responsible government does and then follows up with the implementation of the recommendations. As someone who lives in BC and has seen the price of a starter home in Victoria rise to begin at $750,000, it begs the question why the Federal Government has not done anything to speak of about this issue since it is putting the price of some housing well beyond the reach of Canadians and creating ever increasing numbers of homeless. There was a report a few days ago that stated that rents in Vancouver and Victoria had increased by 20% in six months. Do you think pension, or disability cheques increased by even 1%? You get the picture!

---

38   Professor Maureen Maloney, Professor Tsur Somerville, Professor Brigitte Unger. *Combatting Money Laundering in BC Real Estate*. March 31, 2019.

The legitimacy to govern involves creating safeguards to address issues like money laundering so that housing is more affordable and that Canada is not viewed as a haven for criminal activity by organized crime and others who have illegally gained funds that they wish to have laundered.

I was talking with another writer in Victoria about writing a book about the housing situation in BC. He asked me if I had been downtown at night recently. I said that I hadn't. He then said that the next time I go downtown at night to look at all the new condo buildings and I will see that some hardly have any lights on because they were built with laundered money and the point of them is not to create housing, but rather to launder money in a city desperate for housing. In yet, over seven years the Liberal Government has done very little, as is true in many other areas. Prime Minister Trudeau has always talked a good game but when it comes to rolling up his sleeves and getting something done, he has often fallen woefully short. The following is a letter to the former BC Minister of Finance, Carole James, from the group that created the report on how to combat money laundering in BC real estate. British Columbia recognized this problem and has implemented some measures to address it. For any approach to be effective there must be Federal and Provincial cooperation and the resources necessary to investigate who, how and through what shell companies, and others, money is being laundered.

March 31, 2019 Honourable Carole James Minister of Finance and Deputy Premier PO BOX 9048 STN PROV GOVT Victoria BC V8W 9E2

Dear Minister, It is with great pleasure that we provide you with our report, Combating Money Laundering in BC Real Estate, which recommends improved regulatory measures to enhance the government response to money laundering in real estate in British Columbia. Money laundering is an urgent issue, but not just in BC. It requires concerted federal and provincial efforts to overcome the barriers that currently hold back an effective criminal justice and regulatory response in Canada. International best practices clearly illustrate that we can do better. Through beneficial ownership disclosure, the elimination of regulatory gaps, upgrades to federal anti-money laundering legislation and practices, and better data sharing, coordination and cooperation among agencies, a more effective federal/provincial anti-money laundering regime will be built. Success requires that governments make this a priority, work together and be willing to allocate the necessary resources to ensure successful implementation. Thank you for the opportunity to contribute to resolving this important public policy issue.

Sincerely, Professor Maureen Maloney Chair Professor Tsur Somerville Professor Brigitte Unger.[39]

While BC is starting to tackle the problem, little has been done at a Federal level even though it is a well known fact that money laundering is hurting huge numbers of Canadians by contributing to housing prices few can afford.

Last month, a sweeping report came out which underscores Ottawa's failure. Entitled "Acres of Money Laundering," it was published by Global Financial Integrity

---

39   Professor Maureen Maloney, Professor Tsur Somerville, Professor Brigitte Unger. *Combatting Money Laundering in BC Real Estate.* March 31, 2019.

(GFI) in Washington D.C., the world's foremost think tank on illicit financial flows, corruption, illicit trade, and money laundering. It examines 35 cases in Canada, the tip of the iceberg. Background to this is that I have written dozens of columns about "snow washing" or the flow of billions of dollars of dirty money into Canadian real estate. Ottawa has ignored these as well as recommendations made by GIF and the Financial Action Task Force (FATF) such as requiring lawyers, real estate professionals, mortgage brokers, or notaries to alert authorities to suspicious buyers, lenders, borrowers, or transactions. Canada, except for B.C., has also failed to require that beneficial owners of real estate assets are disclosed publicly. Only in the last budget was a registry announced but it was incomplete and postponed, strangely, until next year or so. GIF's report analyzed the 35 cases involving US$626.3 million in laundered funds over five years. (A 2019 report by the RCMP estimated that C$46.7 billion was laundered in Canada in 2018 alone.) "The laundered money came from drug trafficking in 58.5 percent of the cases. Top foreign origins were China (22.85 per cent), the U.S. (11.4 per cent), Republic of Congo (8.5 per cent) and the rest divided amongst Chad, Mexico, Colombia, Malaysia, Russia and Libya," read the report. "Enablers were: 22.8 percent lawyers; 14.2 percent real estate agents; 11.4 percent real estate development companies and the rest scattered among financial institutions, cryptocurrency outfits, property managers, accountants, and mortgage brokers." Some 88 percent of purchases were residential, 20 percent commercial and, unique to Canada, five per cent agricultural land. Money laundering "typologies" included 51.4 percent anonymous company structures; 45.7 percent third party accessories; 34.2 per cent mortgage schemes; 17.1 percent private loans; 5.7 percent renovations; and 5.7 percent leasing schemes. Also some used the immigrant investor program or overvaluation of property schemes (overpaying to pay off the seller tax-free), said the report. Instead of cracking down on professionals or immigration investor scams, Trudeau announces he will ban blind bids, which keeps buyers from seeing others' offers to "crack down on predatory speculators." He's also threatened to ban foreign buyers for two years which will be pointless given that Canada's a secrecy haven, thanks to its legal, finance, and real estate professionals. Both ideas are useless.[40]

So, as you can see, rather than playing a leadership role and protecting Canadians from money laundering, Trudeau proposes to take measures that are essentially useless. The provinces can do their part but need the Federal Government to do theirs. The fact that this problem has mushroomed to the point that it has speaks to government incompetence. Kids in Victoria are sleeping in vans and tents attending university but the Federal government does nothing. It is pathetic and speaks to Trudeau's incompetence and lack of legitimacy to govern. Housing has been a massive problem in this country for ages and Trudeau has contributed to it by doing so little. It is a sad state of affairs and the sooner we get a Federal

---

40   Diane Francis. Financial Post. *Diane Francis: Trudeau's housing plan won't stop money laundering from fuelling out-of-control prices.* September 3, 2021.

Government that will take serious measures to deal with money laundering and affordable housing for the young and old the better. Canada may gain back some international respect if this happens and may actually have a housing market where both young and old can afford housing. I believe it is too late, however, when a starter home in Victoria is $750,000 and it is worse in Vancouver and Toronto. This type of negligence should be accompanied by some way in which the public can force the issue. I suppose the question that needs to be asked is why the Canadian government has not dealt with this issue in a serious comprehensive way when the Liberal Government has been in power for seven years?

Where to From Here?

IT'S NOT HARD to imagine a stadium filled with tens of thousands of young people cheering wildly. But, before 2015, it would have been difficult to imagine them cheering for anything other than a pop star or sports team, let alone a dishevelled seventy-four-year-old man ranting about campaign-finance reform.

Yet that's exactly what happened when Bernie Sanders crossed America like a rock star, waving his hands in the air while declaring, "We need to get big money out of politics and restore our democracy to combat a corrupted political system controlled by deep-pocketed special interests and the billionaire class."

Sanders was tapping into a fear held by citizens across the Western world: that our elections barely matter anymore because a handful of very wealthy people behind the scenes have much more influence than we do. This sense of political hijacking feeds our growing cynicism towards politics in general, and Sanders figured out how to turn that cynicism into both anger and hope, mobilizing passionate citizens from coast to coast. Here in Canada, corporate influence on democracy is as old as our political system itself. Our very first prime minister, Sir John A. Macdonald, resigned in disgrace after newspapers revealed that he'd not only accepted a bribe but actively pursued it. A political "donation" of $360,000 had apparently been made in exchange for a promised multi-million-dollar contract to build Canada's first transcontinental railroad. The public backlash was swift, leading not only to Macdonald's resignation but to the collapse of his Conservative government.

Bribery is still a part of Canadian politics today, at all three levels of government. (To learn more, Google any of these phrases: *MFP scandal*, *Airbus affair*, *Charbonneau Commission*, or *Gomery report*.) But stories of politicians or political staffers explicitly breaking rules for their own self-interest represent only the tip of the iceberg and are arguably a distraction from the bigger picture. The primary problem we're facing isn't criminal activity but rather the fact that excessive private influence has become a normal and legal part of our system. To put it more bluntly, our political system has evolved into a sophisticated enabler of institutionalized mass, bribery. In just the past couple of years, for example, we saw an enormous public outcry against "cash for access" fundraisers, where wealthy donors schmooze with ministers and parliamentarians in exchange for a hefty fee. The parties of Justin Trudeau, former Ontario premier Kathleen Wynne, and former BC premier Christy Clark in particular were publicly shamed, and each was pressured to introduce legislation designed to limit or minimize these kinds of exchanges. You'd think that 150 years after Macdonald's Pacific Scandal, we'd have this figured out.[41]

---

41   Dave Meslin. The Walrus. *Why bribery still works in Canadian politics.* December 16, 2019.

We could figure it out very easily but figuring it out and there being the political will to bite the hand that feeds them is a completely different matter. Full disclosure of all donations, regardless of the avenues they flow through, of which there are many, would assist, but there must also be maximum contribution levels that can be received in total. Anything exceeding these totals should have to be documented and either returned to the donor, or provided to charity. The problem here is not the complexity of the problem but the strong sense of entitlement and lack of respect for democracy and the constituent. The political will to protect and save democracy is lacking and there is a price to be paid, albeit incrementally. Seattle has a very good solution to this problem that I will discuss shortly. So, it is not as though there are no models out there that have been shown to work in stopping the wealthy from basically buying elections. In the following passage money is being referred to as water in a good analogy.

> Because there are so many routes for the water to travel, you can see how hard it is to try to control the flow of corporate money into our political system with valves alone. That's why many campaign-finance reforms often focus not on how much money is

flowing but on the transparency of the flow. Disclosure regulations force candidates to publicly share detailed information about how much water they have and which pipes it came through. Remember the cash-for-access scandals? Of the three parties involved, only one (the Ontario Liberals) agreed to ban these shady gatherings and completely close that particular valve. The other two parties (the federal Liberals and the BC Liberals) simply added new rules to increase disclosure and transparency. Essentially, they said, "We're still going to sell access to politicians, but we'll put a water metre on it."[42]

Buying access to politicians just clearly shows that the rich are given special privilege and that the Constitution means very little to the corrupt. Since when did a constituent have to buy access to a politician to be heard? I do know that many politicians no longer respond to their constituents. Their claim that they are too busy is a bit ridiculous when you consider that in a democracy there should be no one

------

42   Dave Meslin. The Walrus. *Why bribery still works in Canadian politics.* December 16, 2019

more important to account to than the constituent. I am fortunate to have a Member of Parliament and MLA who have excellent office staff and who are very helpful. I have sent many letters to Trudeau's Ministers asking about things like Can Arrive and other matters and only once have I received a response. Is this because I am not a donor, a corporation, or a lobby group? I don't know but I cannot get a simple email back to a simple question asked in a respectful way. Maybe it is because unlike Trudeau making a big deal about responding to some girl on Facebook there would be no theatrical value in having an aid respond to me. Or perhaps it is because I do not donate to the party. I don't know but that is not accountability.

THE MOST IMPORTANT fix doesn't involve valves or metres. Election campaigns are expensive, and that money has to come from somewhere. Campaigns need fuel—fuel for advertising, printing, polling, office rent, and staff salaries. Rich folks have fuel. Large companies have fuel. We'll never be able to eliminate their desire to influence the political process, but we can displace the need for political donations in the first place by filling the pipes with clean fuel.

Injecting clean, tax-funded fuel into election campaigns shouldn't be controversial. We already publicly fund almost every aspect of elections anyway: the printing of ballots, hiring of election staff, purchasing of tabulation machines, renting of voting stations, and so on. Every single part of our elections is funded by you and me—except for the most important part: the actual campaigns! The best model I've seen for clean campaign fuel is a bold experiment taking place in Seattle: coupons called Democracy Dollars. Four coupons, each worth $25 of public money, are mailed to every voter to give to the candidate(s) of their choice. This system puts complete control of the public subsidy into the hands of all voters, on a level playing field. It's the only system that allows all voters, regardless of disposable income, to participate equally in an election campaign. It provides candidates with a unique incentive to knock on doors and talk to voters. Rather than perpetuating the inertia of the status quo, these dollars can work to amplify new and emerging voices.

In 2017, Seattle's first time trying this new system, the number of campaign donors tripled and reached an all-time high. An estimated 84 percent of the donors were new to the political process, and donors were much more reflective of the general population (with more donations coming from youth, women, people of colour, and low-income residents). The previous election was dominated by big money, and less than 50 percent of total donations came from small contributions. But in 2017, that number had jumped to 87 percent.[43]

Canada could choose to follow the Seattle model being used to level the donor playing field. The problem is that for those who are benefiting from doing favours and backroom deals, fairness has no appeal. Fairness does not result in transactional relationships, or getting one's palms greased. I think Seattle has a wonderful model that I would love to see implemented in Canada at all levels of government. The wealthy would not like the Seattle model because it means they would have the same degree of

---

43 Dave Meslin. The Walrus. *Why bribery still works in Canadian politics.* December 16, 2019

political clout as a poor person. Many wealthy believe that money should entitle them to benefits others do not enjoy, beyond those purchased outside of politics. These are things like influence, political favouritism, nepotism and a host of other things. I believe in equality because I believe in the Canadian Constitution.

It saddens me to see the Canadian and American governments doing so little to protect democracy. There needs to be accountability and stopping the concept of buying access to politicians which is a glorified way of saying, giving the rich special access. The poor cannot indulge in these sorts of transactional relationships because they have nothing to give in return for favours, or special treatment. That is not the way democracy should work. Perhaps this buying access to politicians has appeal to some because it serves to silence groups like the homeless, veterans, the disabled, the impoverished, the young and many members of minority groups. They do not have the money to be heard in this corrupt buy access to a politician process. I find it interesting that all the buying access to politicians' schemes across the country noted above involved the Liberal party.

The ideal is not possible but there are a huge number of measures that can be taken, and, in particular in view of the Trump years where measures can be put into place to curtail similar abuses through severe penalties for those who engage in them. There are those that would argue that the consequences for crimes and ethical violations by politicians should be meted out at the ballot box. This may be true to an extent but let's not confuse elections with criminality. If an employee at McDonald's empties the till their boss does not say that the issue will be brought up on their next performance appraisal. No, they act to deal with the issue now, in the same way that the law must be applied to all who break it. Ethical violations and actions that put the country in a bad light, but are not technically illegal also require harsh consequences, in the same way the Trudeau government was happy to tell us about the $750,000 and $1 million-dollar fines related to Covid-19 quarantine abuses. Trudeau also brought in Emergency Measures, so he is not new to levying severe and extreme responses to things the government deems inappropriate. All I am suggesting is that measures in the same realm of severity be applied to corrupt politicians.

Stopping the Bleeding

I guess I feel embarrassed by the Canadian government scandals that have been commonplace under the Liberal government. I was embarrassed when the Prime Minister's itinerary claimed he was in private meetings in Ottawa and he skipped a critical First Nation's function where approximately 200 children's skeletal remains were found. He opted for a trip to Tofino instead. He should have gone to the First Nation on Canada's first National Day for Truth and Reconciliation. To not go was a slap in the face of all Canada's aboriginal people and showed a callousness I had not seen before from the Prime Minister. As usual the Prime Minister apologized as he did after his two ethical violations. It wears very thin after a while. Canada, under Trudeau has lost a lot of credibility and if you look beyond the legitimacy to govern being more than simply winning enough seats, Trudeau has failed Canada miserably and has lost the legitimacy to govern. He has done far more harm to Canada and its international reputation than good. He talks a lot but produces little. He lacks ethics and has a strong sense of entitlement. He has done little over seven years to deal with the housing crisis, which in a major way is being caused by dirty money being laundered in Canada.

Canada has, once again, slipped down an international ranking for corruption, standing at 13th in the world and well behind world leaders, such as Denmark, New Zealand and Singapore.

Since 2015, the year Liberal leader Justin Trudeau became Prime Minister, Canada has fallen nine points, to a score of 74 out of 100 on the Transparency International 2021 Corruption Perceptions Index. No country has seen a bigger drop in ratings since 2017 than Canada.

While the latest ranking is Canada's worst in a decade, the country remained at the top of the rankings in the Americas, where progress on stamping out corruption has "ground to a halt" and democracies like Chile and the United States rank even lower.

Transparency International, a non-profit non-government organization dedicated to sunshine laws, specifically cited ethical breaches by former Finance Minister Bill Morneau for awarding the administration of a $900 million grants program to WE Charity, which has a history of paying politicians and family members, including the Trudeaus, for speaking events.

Also cited is the SNC-Lavalin "foreign bribery case that spiraled into a political crisis" when Trudeau breached conflict of interest rules by improperly pressuring then-Attorney General Jody Wilson-Raybould to defer prosecution of the construction company.

Transparency International notes how "top-scoring countries," such as Canada, "have proven too weak to meet the challenge of increasingly globalised, networked corruption – which is not measured by the Index.

"As a result, these seemingly 'clean' countries are enabling or even fuelling cross-border corruption, even if it may originate from other places further down the CPI table."[44]

I wrote this book because I am angry about the country I have lived in all these years, being embarrassed internally and externally. I am tired of Prime Minister Trudeau showing a lack of judgement, playing Mr. Costumes when in other countries, being heavy handed with Canadians but hiding when the anti-vaccine rules convoy went to Ottawa. It made me angry that First Nations were so blatantly disrespected when they were unearthing children's graves and that he could not be bothered to show up to the first National Day for Truth and Reconciliation after all that our Indigenous people have gone through. I am tired of the insincere apologies and repeated errors that show a lack of common sense and good judgement.

I am tired of what politics has become and want to see my daughter, her husband and my granddaughter enjoy the same pride in being Canadian that I have up until the Harper and Trudeau years. Harper was a better Prime Minister but went on a power trip

---

44   Graeme Wood. BIV. *Corruption in Canada worst in a decade, finds international watchdog.* January 28, 2022.

and became quite autocratic as right-wing leaders are apt to do. He did not embarrass the country internationally and had far more education and substance than Trudeau. I am left-wing so when I say that you know the present situation is dire. I would like to get back to our peacekeeping role, being viewed as one of the top countries in the world when it comes to not having corruption and being a friend and helper to less fortunate countries and those in dire need. I am pleased we have, and continue to help Ukraine. If we deal with the money laundering issue, we may be able to deal with some of the Russian money being laundered in Canada and that may be a good way to help Ukraine also. I suppose I miss the days of not agreeing ideologically with politicians but having little doubt about their integrity. The past seven years have been ridiculous and I hope we will have ethical inspired, intelligent leadership in the future. I would like to see Canada get back to being part of the solution and stop our decline in the eyes of the world and that means getting a leader of action who does a whole lot more than talk.